This is number one hundred and ninety-five
in the second numbered series
of the Miegunyah Volumes
made possible by the Miegunyah Fund
established by bequests under the wills of
Sir Russell and Lady Grimwade.

'Miegunyah' was Russell Grimwade's home from 1911 to 1955
and Mab Grimwade's home from 1911 to 1973.

MY FORESTS

JANINE BURKE

Travels with Trees

THE MIEGUNYAH PRESS

THE MIEGUNYAH PRESS
An imprint of Melbourne University Publishing Limited
Level 1, 715 Swanston Street, Carlton, Victoria 3053, Australia
mup-contact@unimelb.edu.au
www.mup.com.au

First published 2021
Text © Janine Burke, 2021
Design and typography © Melbourne University Publishing Limited, 2021

Typeset in Bembo 12/15pt by Cannon Typesetting
Cover design by Pfisterer + Freeman
Printed in China by 1010 Printing Asia Ltd

 A catalogue record for this
book is available from the
National Library of Australia

9780522877328 (hardback)
9780522877335 (ebook)

Contents

ELWOOD, MY FOREST

Y OU MIGHT BE wondering why an art historian is writing about trees. For those of you familiar with *Nest: The art of birds* (2012), it's clear how this book came about. It grew from there. (Excuse the pun!) To spend time observing birds and nests is to spend time observing trees, especially those in Elwood, my neighbourhood, near Melbourne in south-eastern Australia. It made me realise how ignorant I was of their histories and journeys, of the extent of their impact on human and non-human cultures. How much we need them. If only the birds could answer our questions about trees! Their knowledge would be massive, detailed and practical, stretching beyond human memory.

I'm not a country girl. I grew up in suburbia. So, like most people on the planet, my daily contact with nature is conditioned by urban planning, population demands and pollution. My environment is designed. I learn from what is around me and when I can visit wild places, it's the opportunity to gaze into the past, at what my country once looked like. But that, too, is influenced by human occupation which began around sixty thousand years ago when Indigenous people, those brave pioneers, arrived here, all the way from Africa. They also designed nature.

Writing this book, my tree-memories began to return, a kind of botanical autobiography that anyone who admires trees is certain to have—the Eucalypt that grew outside my bedroom window and to whom, as an intense, imaginative seventeen-year-old, I confided my hopes and fears. The Olive grove that surrounded the house where I lived in Tuscany: it was as though the trees had been dancing and the moment of discovery froze them. Horse-chestnuts blooming in glorious fecundity along the boulevards of Paris. The Canary Island Palms of St Kilda, Elwood's raffish neighbour, that give the suburb its tropical holiday air.

As American essayist Oliver Wendell Holmes noted, 'I have a most intense, passionate fondness for trees in general, and have had several romantic attachments to certain trees in particular.'[1] If those sentiments strike a chord, please wander with me through forests, art and writing, civilisations—some past, some continuous—cities and parks, swamps and sewers, around our globe, this precious Earth whom the trees help to breathe.

Let's start in Elwood.

When you turn into Elwood from Nepean Highway, you are embraced by green: the parks and the ovals entwine in flowing emerald arcs like large, protective gestures. It's like living in a nature reserve. The trees assist in giving Elwood its decidedly feminine air, its gentle, verdant appeal. Elwood is inhabited by a wide variety of trees: Eucalypts as well as Wattle, Bottlebrush, Ti-tree, Banksia, Apple, Sheoak, Moreton Bay Fig, Jacaranda, Pine, Ash, Peppercorn, Cypress, Date Palm, Silver Birch, Elm and London Plane. My Elwood forest is an urban hybrid. You've probably noticed that I've capitalised the trees' names. I think it's fitting. That is, after all, what they're called. You wouldn't like it if, for example, you were called Jane Doe but I referred to you as jane doe. Some trees are already thus endowed but I feel they all deserve such distinction. Trees have evolved over millennia long before *Homo sapiens* and they continue to try to adjust to whatever we expect of them. They are history, growing before our very eyes. If that perspective annoys you ('anthropomorphism' I hear some of you muttering), you may not like the rest of this book and perhaps should desist from reading on.

Elwood ends at Port Phillip Bay, our placid sea, our aquamarine zone. In the distance, to the south, is Mount Martha and beyond that the distant Heads. Facing Elwood across the bay are the You Yangs, a series of granite ridges rising from a treeless plain near Geelong.

On the Point Ormond bluff which commands that view, the Yaluk-ut Weelam people of the Boonwurrung clans once harvested shellfish, hunted and camped.[2] It was also an excellent surveillance site. Yaluk-ut Weelam means 'river home' or 'river people'.[3] Thomas Clark's painting *Red Bluff, Elwood* (c. 1860, National Gallery of Victoria), as Point Ormond was then known, shows the golden-pink sandstone cliffs. When Clark painted the bluff, much of Elwood was a swamp.

Red Bluff, Elwood, c. 1860, Thomas Clark, oil on canvas, 47.2 × 91.5 cm, National Gallery of Victoria, Melbourne, Gift of Marilyn Leonie Kino through the Australian Government's Cultural Gifts Program, 2016.

It had been a paradise for the Yaluk-ut Weelam. The wet-
lands provided a rich abundance of food not only for that clan
but for others who passed through, a feast of ducks, eels, tortoises,
frogs and fish. Kangaroos and emus were plentiful and provided
another food source. When the area flooded, the Yaluk-ut
Weelam moved to higher ground where they continued to reap,
in an environmentally conscious and adept way, the best the land
had to offer.

Several of Elwood's mighty Eucalypts, the sentinels of the
suburb, grew along the wetland's higher ground and flourish
still. Drooping Sheoaks (*Allocasuarina verticillata*) provided timber
needed for hunting implements and weapons. Today, sheltered
behind Point Ormond are many original plant species including
Sea Box (*Alyxia buxifolia*), White Correa (*Correa alba*) and Coastal
Daisy Bush (*Olearia axillaris*), flourishing reminders of the Yaluk-ut
Weelam's reign.[4]

Ironically, it was the expert land management practised by
Aboriginal people that made it so attractive to property-hungry
settlers. As Bill Gammage notes in *The Biggest Estate on Earth:
How Aborigines Made Australia*, early explorers commented on the
orderly appearance of some parts of the land. In 1770, Sydney
Parkinson, the botanical artist on board HMS *Endeavour* with
Lieutenant James Cook, wrote of Botany Bay, 'The country looked
very pleasant and fertile; and the trees, quite free from underwood,
appeared like plantations in a gentleman's park.'[5] Who better than
an artist to assess the country's aesthetic qualities? Its 'look' was due
to Indigenous people who practised firestick farming, using fire as
an ally in clearing and maintaining the bush.

In 1839, William Thomas was appointed as an assistant protector of the Yaluk-ut Weelam, among other Aboriginal clans, in the
Port Phillip District, as Victoria was then known. Thomas was a
teacher and a devout Methodist. He observed,

> They are generous among themselves. Those who are fortu-
> nate through the day will distribute amongst those who are

unsuccessful. Those who are ill are not expected to tramp through the bush for food. If children are left orphans those children [are] … supported among them … A child of three is capable of getting their portion in collecting gum etc., They live in the greatest harmony among themselves.[6]

Such charitable and perceptive opinions were rare.

Catastrophe and white settlement went hand in hand. In 1835, John Batman dropped anchor at what would later be known as Elwood. He'd arrived from Launceston on his schooner *Rebecca* before sailing up the Yarra River in a bid to establish the site of Melbourne. The artist John Glover was Batman's neighbour back in the north of Van Diemen's Land. They lived in the foothills of Ben Lomond. Glover was an English painter of inspired and elegant landscapes who had settled in his new home in 1832. His work often included beautifully realised studies of Aboriginal people depicting them as a vital and intrinsic part of the land. It was an unusual subject in white Australian art. Glover considered Batman 'a rogue, thief, cheat and liar, a murderer of blacks and the vilest man I have ever known'.[7]

Batman was responsible for hunting down and killing Aboriginal people in what became known as the Black War. It made him quite a hero in Van Diemen's Land. Batman enlisted Aboriginal men from New South Wales to assist him as trackers. He also deployed them in government-authorised 'roving parties' (contingents of armed bounty hunters) that operated in north-west Tasmania during the period of martial law from late 1828 to early 1832. During that time Batman is known to have led a massacre of Aboriginal people in the Ben Lomond foothills.[8]

In Batman's forays into Port Phillip District, he adopted a more diplomatic approach. He was courteous and respectful. He befriended senior Aboriginal men including Derrimut, leader of the Yaluk-ut Weelam. Not only did Derrimut warn Batman that other Aboriginal clans were preparing to attack him and his men, he also tried to save Batman's son from drowning. The incongruity of an Aboriginal man offering assistance to one who had murdered many of his people beggars description.

Famously, Batman sought to strike a treaty with Aboriginal clans.[9] But he was thwarted by the government who rejected the treaty and declared the land terra nullius. It meant the government could turn real estate agent, disregard Indigenous concerns and profit handsomely from the hundreds of settlers who poured into Port Phillip District eager to buy.

What did this mean for Elwood? European illnesses, like smallpox, dysentery, syphilis, typhoid and influenza, contributed to the deaths of many Indigenous people. In 1840, the *Glen Huntley* arrived at Point Ormond, flying the fever flag, and Victoria's first quarantine station was established there as a result. Equally devastating was the introduction of sheep and cattle. In 1836, sheep had begun grazing at Red Bluff, occupying traditional lands and destroying much of the native vegetation like the Yam Daisy (*Microseris lanceolata*) from whose edible roots the Yaluk-ut Weelam made bread. By 1839 Benjamin Baxter, Melbourne's first post-master, was grazing cattle on his lease of land from Port Ormond to Port Melbourne, a huge swathe of territory that belonged—and continues to belong—to the Yaluk-ut Weelam.[10]

Trees were felled for buildings, firewood and other needs. In Clark's *Coastal Scene, St Kilda* (1857, National Gallery of Victoria) a man leads a team of oxen carrying a load of freshly cut timber. It situates tree felling, literally and symbolically, as the crux of the composition.

Clark's *Red Bluff, Elwood* further explores the change. In the foreground two fishermen casually lean against their boat as one smokes his pipe. The work of the day is done and it's time to relax. Next to the boat is a crayfish pot for catching shellfish, a task once acquitted by women members of the Yaluk-ut Weelam. A black and white cat sits nearby, attentively observing the men and no doubt eyeing their catch for a feed. It seems a charming and innocent scene yet it shows how white settlement quickly and irrevocably changed the business of land management.

The 'whiteness' of Clark's landscape obliterates the blackness of its past. In a sense, it's a cemetery. Aboriginal rights were buried there.

When William Thomas was appointed, he recorded that the number of Boonwurrung, which had been around three hundred, was reduced to eighty-three people.[11] By 1857, the members of the Boonwurrung and the neighbouring clan Woi Wurrung comprised a total of twenty-eight people, with only eleven remaining Boonwurrung.[12] The latter was practising birth control: why have many children when they could no longer inherit their ancestral lands? A brutal process of resettlement began as the Yaluk-ut Weelam were forcibly removed from their home territories. Each time they were moved—for example to Mordialloc, further down the bay—settlers would lust after that land, too, and another relocation would take place as the clans were shunted from one end of Port Phillip District to the other.

No wonder Derrimut confronted William Thomas, asking why 'white man take away Mordialloc where black fellows always sit down'.[13] Thomas was in agreement with Derrimut but could do nothing to shift the often obdurate and bigoted attitudes that informed government policy. Poor Derrimut. Perhaps it was only later he realised that Batman and the other whitefellas had not sought to honour and assist him but to destroy his way of life, and him with it. He died in 1864, at the Melbourne Benevolent Asylum for the destitute, a broken man.

Fortunately, we have a tree memorial to the Yaluk-ut Weelam. I went to visit it on a mild afternoon in late summer. It's a River Red Gum (*Eucalyptus camaldulensis*), perhaps three hundred to five hundred years old, known as the Ngargee, or Corroboree, Tree beneath which, for centuries, the Yaluk-ut Weelam gathered and performed ceremonies. It survives, a proud old giant, near a cluster of frantic traffic routes in St Kilda, reminding us that behind the 'civilisation' of white settlement a connection with place continues.[14] Hopefully, over time, it's a connection that will become ever more precious and emphatic. Evocatively, local

historian Meyer Eidelson describes the Ngargee Tree as 'the oldest living resident' of the area.[15] It was once part of a forest.

I parked my car in Fitzroy Street and crossed the reserve, carved out with walking paths, before entering a sequestered area, landscaped with native grasses and flowering plants, and arranged with low wooden benches. Sitting there, in the presence of the tree, I felt I was living in two time zones at once. First, there was the noise and buzz of the traffic, the crescendo of modern life, and the sight of a tall building vaulting behind the tree. Then there was the stillness and 'otherness' of the River Red Gum and its bush surround, the calm *being* of the place.

Where I sat, so had the Yaluk-ut Weelam, men and women wearing cosy, honey-coloured possum-skin cloaks to keep out the cold. Preparing the food, perhaps a feast of oysters and cray-fish, and kangaroo meat roasted over the fire, and freshly baked bread. Children playing. Later there would be dance and song, laughter and storytelling. Settling down at night, the people saw the sky spangled with the glittering jewels of the Milky Way, the constellations which told creation stories about mythic beings, and the seasons.

If the Ngargee Tree is between three hundred and five hundred years old, then it was growing when Michelangelo had not long finished painting the Sistine Chapel and Ferdinand Magellan was setting sail from Spain to circumnavigate the globe. Is it possible to time travel? Sitting there, imagining myself to be surrounded by the spirits of the Yaluk-ut Weelam, I glimpsed their way of life and their careful treatment of the land. The people do not own the land, the saying goes, the land owns the people. The Ngargee Tree helps me to view that past. In fact, the Eucalypt represents it, as do other venerable trees in the neighbourhood. They are the memories of Aboriginal people emblematised. They remind, this is Aboriginal land.

Ngargee or Corroboree Tree, St Kilda, Janine Burke, 2020.

Elwood has not always been arboreally opulent. Meyer Eidelson, who grew up here in the 1970s, recalls that parts of the suburb, like the Point Ormond beachfront where the Yaluk-ut Weelam had camped, were treeless and dry. The environmental group Earthcare, founded in 1989, had a mission to plant as many trees as possible. Eidelson, a member of Earthcare, reckons it was 'well over a million'. That project not only provided welcome shade but decisively changed Elwood's climate, which has become 'more temperate, cooler and moist'.[16]

But there was one tree that populated this place and which can be seen in profusion in a 1937 aerial photograph. The London Plane (*Platanus* × *acerifolia*) is Elwood's best represented non-native tree, and an iconic feature. It's in most streets, no matter how narrow, giving Elwood the impression of an oasis, a serene island between the roaring highway and the more ordinary suburbs nearby, congested with tram and train lines.

A London Plane is one of the reasons I made my home here. From my study, where I'm now sitting, it's two house-blocks away, a grand being about 20 metres tall and with a crown 10 metres wide, always busy with birds and the wind. When I first inspected my apartment and saw the tree and knew that I would see it every day that I wrote, it spurred my decision. Of course, I live in dread that a new neighbour might treat it as a hazard and cut it down. But, perhaps like me, my neighbours continue to regard the tree as a treasure and an inspiration. It has never disappointed me.

There's another Plane that stands directly in front of my apartment block whose branches reach out in a leisurely fashion to stroke those of its fellows. Its dappled trunk is a delicately hued palette: an underskin of pastel pink, where the bark has shed and which looks as tender as flesh, then robust layers of olive-green and mauve-grey bark, the latter almost iridescent, while its top skin is scabrous and leaden coloured. In sunshine, the tree's wide leaves create a shifting green and gold luminescence, quite dazzling to behold. In the afternoons, when the southerly sweeps down

London Plane bark, Elwood, Janine Burke, 2019.

St Kilda Street from the sea, the leaves rustle as if conversing in some ancient, subtle language that perhaps humans once understood. Perhaps the birds still do.

Native birds have taken to this northern hemisphere foreigner. Further up the street, a Willie Wagtail couple built a confection of twigs and spider silk high in the branches. It proved a sturdy home as, during one spring and into the summer, Mr and Mrs Wagtail successfully brooded three clutches, one after another, eight babies in all, who could be seen bouncing up and down in the nest and, with pleasure and wonder, stretching their wings. The parents' sharp, tiny faces and long tail-feathers protruded from the nest and, on days when the boughs dipped and rocked in the wind, the birds breasted the force with all the confidence of a captain on the prow. Magpie Larks, too, choose the Plane trees for their solid mud constructions, though they typically opt for the bare, forked branch of a Eucalypt.

One evening in late summer, a flock of Corellas arrived, about two hundred strong, and threw a party in the park opposite that lasted all night and kept us awake. I'd never seen such a contingent in Elwood before. Though the Little Corellas favoured the River Red Gum in which to roost, it was the Plane trees they were after. The trees produce a fruit, though that word does not adequately evoke the small, hard, spiky, green globe that the trees bear. I have never seen a bird show the slightest interest in them but, for the parrots, it was a feast. They shrieked with glee as they munched on the fruit, which they dropped to the ground after a few mouthfuls. Soon the sidewalk and the road were littered with thousands of little green balls as well as a thick scattering of dusty, downy seeds. It was as if a giant had walked down the street, grabbing the trees and shaking them.

When the Corellas had eaten their fill, they moved off in a mob to other streets, other branches, screaming out their good fortune. There seemed no explanation for their appearance. Had a drought up north sent them searching for food far from their usual habitat? How did they know the banquet was there, ripe for the picking?

At first thrilled and astonished by their presence, we gradually began to resent them: the mess, the noise. It was easy to skid on the broken fruit. The air was dense with seeds. We sneezed. The Corellas perched in the trees and pooed on the pavement. Looking up, it seemed the branches were crowded with white ornaments. When were these guys going to leave?

Plane trees, too, can be unwanted guests. Though in autumn it's fun to stride through the dry, burnished stacks of leaves, crunching them underfoot, they accumulate in large piles and the wind is neither strong nor consistent enough to disperse them. The locals, or in my case, the owners' corporation cleaners, need rakes and leaf blowers to clean up. These trees are hardy, they can endure city life. Of course, it's a reason for planting them. It's how they got their name. There's a London Plane not far from the entrance to the Jardin des Plantes in Paris which has been growing there since 1785. Many of its roots have dispensed with the earth and rise, steep and regular as stairs. It has grown so tall its top branches are lost to human view and engage only with the sky.

My pleasure in the Plane outside my apartment block is somewhat tempered by the fact that it recently cost me around five thousand dollars. That's because it doesn't like the strip of earth assigned to it. Not only have its knotted roots broken the footpath, doubling and trebling back on themselves like the writhing body of a giant snake but, to quench the tree's thirst, the roots found, grappled with and finally strangled our sewerage system.

After a week's work removing the roots and replacing the pipes, the crew of six plumbers was baffled, and momentarily vanquished, by the tree. Not only had its fine hair-like roots entered the sewer and matted there but other, larger ones had wrapped themselves around the pipes. The exposed tree-fists were alarming in their fierce, blind inexorability as though a desperate, subterranean strategy had been accidentally brought to light. Unlike us, the tree was not poisoned by our waste but thrived on it, deriving moisture and nutrients. What our bodies discarded made it strong. The plumbers could no longer use the machines that sliced through the ground because they risked severing gas and water pipes. The job had to be done by hand.

The crew was frustrated. So were the residents: we had to fork out more money for the completion of the job. But in the foreman's voice as he explained the dilemma, I detected a hint of admiration. The tree had stood up to him. And, briefly, it had won. Peter Wohlleben in his informative and imaginative book *The Hidden Life of Trees* considers roots the most important part, the tree equivalent of where a brain is located. 'Can [trees] think?' he asks. 'Are they intelligent?'[17] If the Plane's root system could answer, it might be, 'You betcha!'

Closer to my study than either the Plane that brought me here, or the costly one at the front of my apartment building, is a Silver Birch (*Betula pendula*). An exquisite, slender, white creature whose long, drooping branches make it seem as if it is constantly sorrowing, the Birch grows in a small plot in the sideway near the clotheslines. Unlike the Plane, it seems to accept its lot and not rebel against its miserly space. However, I do not trust it. Firstly, I suspect it may be in league with the Plane tree in the destruction of our sewers. Secondly, it's growing capable of breaking my kitchen windows when its branches lash them in a high wind.

Birds alight on the branches of the Silver Birch but do not nest there: it's too exposed. One airless summer night, I wandered into the kitchen for a glass of water to be met by the glassy-eyed gaze of a Ringtail Possum. It was no bigger than a cat with comparably fine fur, and its tail was curled several times around the branch on which it sat. Ringtails nest in trees, the females building communal nurseries known as dreys that are composed of sticks, or, failing that, they simply curl up in a tree's intersecting branches. It's the Brushtail Possum whom you might find an unwelcome visitor in your roof, pissing and staining your ceiling and generally making a ruckus at sunrise when the family comes home from foraging. When possums moved into my roof last winter, the Silver Birch was their ladder.

In forests, the Silver Birch can also act as a nurse log from which other trees, such as Conifers, draw sustenance and grow. Birches were among the first trees to become established after the glaciers receded following the last Ice Age, circa 110 000 to 11 700 years ago. Hardy, quick growing, and relatively immune to disease and insect attack, they are valuable in reforestation and erosion control. But, as Patrick Baker, professor of silviculture and forest ecology at Melbourne University, points out, nurse logs 'are a bit of a Faustian bargain'.[18] While the log may provide a raised site for a new tree to grow on (so it has a height advantage over its neighbours), the nurse log eventually decays and collapses, and any tree growing on top of it risks falling to the ground.

If you find yourself in Finland taking a sauna, the branches with which you thwack yourself will most likely be Silver Birch, the country's national tree. Its fragrant twigs, tied together in a kind of posy, are believed to stimulate and relax the muscles. 'Most beautiful of forest trees,' sighed Samuel Taylor Coleridge, 'the Lady of the Woods.'

There's something else intriguing about Silver Birches that a team of Finnish and Hungarian scientists has recently discovered: they sleep. For the first time, trees have been shown to undergo physical changes at night that can be likened to sleep, or at least to day–night cycles. Branches of birch trees have been seen drooping by as much as 10 centimetres at the tips towards the end of the night. 'It was a very clear effect, and applied to the whole tree,' says András Zlinszky of the Centre for Ecological Research in Tihany, Hungary. 'No one has observed this effect before at the scale of whole trees, and I was surprised by the extent of the changes.'[19] So, shush! Don't disturb the trees. They need their rest.

TREES
AS HOME

ONCE UPON A time, we lived in the trees. It's called arboreality. A lovely word that suggests trees create their own reality which, in a sense, they do. That was before we evolved as *Homo sapiens*, before we climbed down from the branches and left our closest relatives, the chimpanzee and the bonobo, behind. Our genus of hominins evolved about six million years ago. In 1974, in northern Ethiopia, the skeleton of one of our ancestors, *Australopithecus afarensis*, was found. At 3.2 million years old, she is justly famous. Though she is nicknamed Lucy, in Amharic her name is Dinknesh meaning 'you are marvellous'. If you decide to see Lucy's remains, they're on display at the National Museum of Ethiopia in Addis Ababa—well, a plastic replica at least.[1]

Trees were a desirable location in which to reside given the savanna was teeming with Sabre-toothed Cats, 200-kilogram 'bear otters' and huge dog-like creatures.[2] Fortunately, Lucy and her family had shoulder blades that were closer in shape to those of apes than modern humans. It meant they could use their upper limbs for climbing and balancing. Lucy's feet had arches, so she could stand and walk upright, but her upper body strength, and long, dangling arms, meant she could clamber up a tree when she needed to. Lucy resembled a chimpanzee—she was around the same height and weight—and was just as cute.

Which were the trees that sheltered Lucy? Trees have existed before almost any other form of life. Wattieza, the earliest known tree, was recently discovered in upstate New York.[3] It was alive and thriving 385 million years ago, long before the most primitive forms of animals began crawling out of the water. In that lush tropical world, there was no sound except wind and rain. Wattieza's branches resembled a fern, it stood at around 8 metres and looked rather like a Palm tree. Fossilised stumps were found in the 1870s but it was only in 2004 that the pieces of the puzzle literally came together when a team of scientists unearthed a 180-kilogram crown, and then fragments of a trunk.

Wattieza, Illustration 71155849, Corey A. Ford/Dreamstime.com.

As William Stein, a palaeobotanist at the State University of New York at Binghamton commented, 'I don't think any of us dared to think of [the earliest trees] being quite that big.'[4] The Middle Devonian was a time when the first forests were forming, drastically altering the climate, changing Earth's systems and creating environments that encouraged the evolution of terrestrial animals. Forests began to do then what they continue to do— provide canopies of shade and help the planet breathe.

Wattieza, and other trees and plants that began to develop a little later, provide the deposits of fossil fuel that we have come to rely on today, including coal, the mining of which is the most controversial of all climate change issues, especially here in Australia, as we are the third largest exporter of brown coal in the world. In my state, Victoria, coal is the primary energy source used to generate electricity. Over millions of years, the dead Wattiezas and their colleagues formed thick layers of peat which, under pressure from layers of earth built up over time, was turned into coal.

Due to logging, hardly any coal is currently being formed because forests are constantly being cleared. The trees-turned-peat-turned-coal store carbon dioxide and when coal is burned, the carbon dioxide is released into the atmosphere. In large quantities these greenhouse gas emissions are dangerous to all life both because they pollute the air and because they slowly and inexorably raise the Earth's temperature. Carbon emissions constitute one of the greatest risks and challenges facing humanity. The brutal fact is, as Tim Flannery points out, 'even if we ceased burning fossil fuels today, it would take several centuries for life, the oceans and Earth's crust to re-absorb the excess'.[5] It's an issue we'll return to.

While the Hadar region of Ethiopia today is a dry, unforgiving landscape, in Lucy's time it was an open grassland with trees. If Lucy and her family planned to stay for a bit, they'd do what chimpanzees do in the wild: build a nest in a tree by lacing branches together. Lucy would have taught that skill to her children.

The comfortable, loosely woven beds made by chimpanzees consist of a mattress supported on a strong foundation, and are lined with soft leaves and twigs. Both day and night beds are constructed, the former for a siesta. Not only are the beds safer than sleeping on the ground, but they are warmer, and the leaves offer some resistance to insects. The tree where Lucy sought shelter may not have been entirely Sabre-toothed Cat proof but it offered repose as well as a refuge from the dangers below. The dwelling-place of the nomad can only be transitory and, enclosed within her tree, Lucy and her family could, for a while at least, sleep peacefully and dream.

Between fifty to eighty thousand years ago, small groups of our human ancestors left Africa and set off to explore the rest of the world. They might have had little in the way of technology but they were primed with carefully attuned observations of nature, and with fierce, clever hunting skills. Probably in the Middle East some met and made love with Neanderthals. Poor old Neanderthals! They have an entirely undeserved reputation for symbolising stupidity, as in 'What a *Neanderthal*!' The Neanderthals died out and it remains unknown whether that may have been due to *Homo sapiens*.

On their epic journey from Africa, our ancestors followed the coastline, some fanning out across Asia, some making their way to Australia. The latter are the forebears of the Indigenous people of my country whose culture continues in an unbroken line to this day.

When the people reached the Timor Sea, around 90 kilometres from the northern Australian coast, they lashed together rafts of logs, and sailed over. There were probably around ten to twenty people on each raft—the first boat people. That was around sixty thousand years ago. As archaeologist Scott Cane writes, 'it was the first oceanic water crossing in world history'.[6] Those people went sailing into a land rich with fauna, such as giant kangaroos and wombats who, having never encountered *Homo sapiens* before, had no fear of predation. Fish, birds, everything was plentiful in northern Australia.

Over millennia, *Homo sapiens* quit the trees for the earth. But not the Korowai people who live in Indonesian West Papua (formerly Irian Jaya). They have maintained Lucy's tradition. They often choose to be arborealists, perhaps the only ones left on the planet. Their other claim to fame is that they are cannibals. Johannes Veldhuizen, a Dutch priest with the Mission of the Reformed Churches, first made contact with the Korowai in 1978, but dropped plans to convert them to Christianity. The Korowai believed that their gods would turn against them and destroy their world if outsiders changed their customs. However, their resolve seems to have weakened in recent years and the first converts to Christianity were baptised in the late 1990s.

Until Veldhuizen arrived, it was unlikely the Korowai had had much contact with their neighbours, let alone white First World visitors. The Korowai's skill as architects is such that they have attracted the global attention of scientists, journalists and film crews.[7]

The tribe lives in a rainforest where trees grow tall and fast because it's a race to survive, to break through the thick canopy of branches at the top and find clean air and light for photosynthesis. Below is the fetid, muddy, gloomy, bug-laden undergrowth of the tropical forest. The annual rainfall in the area is around 5 metres, making it one of the wettest places on Earth. It's another reason for living in the trees: the area is deluged in the wet season.

The Korowai start the project by selecting a tall tree, often a Banyan (*Ficus benghalensis*) as the central support. The men cut its crown and build the floor on its sturdy trunk, supported by other nearby trees, all cut to equal height. Most treehouses are set around 8 to 10 metres above the ground. The floor is covered with a carpet

Korowai people's home, West Papua, Sergey Uryadnikov/Alamy Stock Photo, 2016.

of the Betel Palm leaf (*Areca catechu*) while the walls are made from the wooden shafts of Sago Palms (*Cycas revoluta*) lashed together with rattan ropes. Leaves or grass stalks are used to cover any holes. That's to keep out demons and witches.[8]

The biggest threat is fire, so the hearth is suspended in a hole in the floor filled with a layer of leaves and clay. If fire escapes the hearth, the hearth is cut free, and falls to the ground.

The treehouse usually lasts about five years. It takes around a fortnight to build and the tribe will enlist the help of their nearest neighbours—a favour that is always returned. The Korowai make it look easy: they sing melodically as they build, and whoop with delight when branches are cut from the tree and crash to the ground.

To watch the Korowai ascend is to observe grace and confidence in motion. The bigger treehouses have areas for men and women, with stairs leading to the sex-segregated sections. The stairs are made from thin poles with notches for the feet. The men have a gallant custom. When the tribe moves in, they climb up first, so when the ladies ascend there's no chance someone might be looking up their skirts.

Everyone lives up there: families, pets such as dogs and pretty little pigs with curly tails that are eaten on special occasions. Parents seem quite relaxed about allowing their children to wander near the platform's edge. Thus the children gain competence in their perilous lifestyle when quite young. No-one leaves the house at night: that's when the nasty spirits are out and about.

In Korowai life and mythology, the tree has a major functioning role. It is the place where they sleep, eat, laugh, make love, prepare food and tell stories. Anthropologist and specialist in Korowai culture Rupert Stasch regards the treehouses as artworks, not only due to their design values, but because the people's lives are a palimpsest, 'poetically superimposed' on the tree/home.[9] The Korowai also measure time by the longevity of the treehouses, giving them 'great significance for the Korowai; in some sense it can be seen as a microcosm in which the clan lives and moves'.[10]

But let's not get too sentimental about the Korowai. Before we bid them farewell, let's take a look at their unpleasant habit of eating one another. It also functions as a graphic description of life within the tree home.

Though this practice is said to have been abandoned, Paul Raffaele, writing for *Smithsonian Magazine*, offers a gripping and unsettling account of his visit to the remote region inhabited by one group of the Korowai. It's a journey into *Heart of Darkness*.

I'll let Raffaele set the scene. Kembaren, his Korowai guide, has led him to a treehouse, after trekking through dense jungle and fording a deep stream.

> I can hear voices as I climb an almost vertical pole notched with footholds. The interior of the treehouse is wreathed in a haze of smoke rent by beams of sunlight. Young men are bunched on the floor near the entrance. Smoke from hearth fires has coated the bark walls and sago-leaf ceiling, giving the hut a sooty odour. A pair of stone axes, several bows and arrows and net bags are tucked into the leafy rafters. The floor creaks as I settle cross-legged onto it.[11]

The group are curious to see their first *laleo*, or ghost-demon, a name used for Europeans. Raffaele spends several days with these Korowai, waiting for them to trust him enough to frankly answer his questions about cannibalism. Then, prior to leaving the area, Raffaele is taken to another treehouse, where his hosts have killed a pig in his honour. Raffaele has clearly been a hit with the locals.

'Inside [the treehouse] every nook and cranny is crammed with bones from previous feasts—spiky fish skeletons, blockbuster pig jaws, the skulls of flying foxes and rats. The bones dangle even from hooks strung along the ceiling, near bundles of many-coloured parrot and cassowary feathers.' The Korowai believe that the decor signals 'hospitality and prosperity'.[12]

The Korowai explain to Raffaele they do not regard their practice as cannibalism but rather as protective magic. The *khakua* is an evil spirit who kills his male prey by devouring him from the inside. As he is dying, the bewitched man whispers the name of the *khakua* to his nearest and dearest. As revenge, that man is obliged to be killed and eaten by his fellow tribe members, no matter how loudly he might protest his innocence.

At the treehouse banquet, Raffaele meets Khandoup who tells him the taste of *khakua* is the most delicious of any creature he's ever eaten. Bailom, the brother of one of Raffaele's porters, pulls from his bag a human skull with a hole bashed in its forehead, his most recent *khakua*. Bailom shows no remorse. 'Revenge is part of our culture,' he comments.[13]

Were the Korowai playing Raffaele for a fool? Playing the age-old game of regaling the susceptible First-Worlder with the tall tales he wants to hear from Indigenous people? Raffaele believes not. Either way, life is perilous for the Korowai—whether it's building a home 8 metres up a tree or surviving the ordeals of witchcraft.

There's not much Miranda Gibson doesn't know about arboreality. In 2011, when she was thirty-one, she climbed 60 metres up a 400-year-old Eucalypt, dubbed the Observer Tree (nice pun!), in Tasmania's southern Tyenna Valley. That's six times the height of the highest Korowai treehouse. She remained there, on a 3-metre-long platform, for the next 449 days. It was a brave and dangerous action to protect the forest, and that particular tree, from clear-felling by loggers. When Miranda descended it wasn't because she'd quailed at the physical and psychological hardships of the task but because a nearby bushfire, which police later informed her had been deliberately lit, threatened her and her support team on the ground.

Watching Miranda clamber up to the tree's canopy, courtesy of the videos made by Gibson and her colleagues from the group

Still Wild, Still Threatened, is to realise what a perilous feat she
undertook.[14] The climb had to be done at night, making it even
more hazardous. That was because Miranda and her team, who
were in the forest constructing the platform and organising her
gear, awoke one morning to the sound of tree-felling. It was mid-
December and the group's information was that logging would not
commence until January. That unexpected turn of events meant
that 'everything speeded up. We had to work day and night. If the
loggers came up the hill and found us, or if the cops had arrived,
it would be over.'[15] So, under cover of darkness, Gibson ascended
and then, with help, hauled the platform and all her gear, including
her composting toilet. The next day, the police arrived but 'I was
already up there and we launched it in the media, so we were really
lucky'.[16] Soon after, the loggers quit the site and did not return.
Already a victory of sorts.

Settling herself on the platform, Miranda chatted into her
camera, legs swinging over that vast space, as cheerful as a kid in a

Miranda Gibson in the Observer Tree, Tyenna Valley, Tasmania, Photographer Unknown, 2012.

playground. Just watching that scene gave me vertigo. Perhaps it's no surprise that Miranda's name is derived from the Latin *mirandus* meaning to be wondered or marvelled at. In *The Tempest* (1611), Shakespeare bestowed the name on the play's only female character, the feisty but compassionate daughter of the magician Prospero. It is she who speaks the play's most famous lines, 'O brave new world. That has such people in't.'

In a televised interview conducted on the platform in 2012, Miranda was calm and articulate. Open-faced with dark eyes and hair, she had a ready, endearing smile: I had the impression of a humble person of immense fortitude. Miranda was grateful, she said, for the opportunity to spend so much time in the forest, 'to witness it. What the trees go through, I go through.'[17] The Observer Tree was chosen because it was at the top of the ridge that overlooks the valley, thus providing a view of where the next round of logging would take place. The outlook is spectacular.

Miranda also noted the birds who came to inspect her. Her best bird friends were the Currawongs who visited daily. Smart birds who are naturally curious, the Currawongs were interested in what Miranda was up to and what new items may have arrived on the platform via the ground support team, perhaps something to eat. From her 'office in the clouds', Miranda recorded the seasons, sunsets and a heavy snow fall, the last of which delighted her.[18]

Miranda had mentally prepared herself as best she could, though it was a situation that was 'completely unpredictable'.[19] Perhaps her sit would last a few months, or perhaps only days if the police decided to climb up and arrest her. She had no idea her stay would last more than a year. The experience of living in the tree's canopy was extraordinary—there were 'the powerful moments of inspiration, to the depths of loneliness and isolation'.[20] She had welcome visits from family members—her father dressed up as Santa Claus for his ascent at Christmas—plus friends, journalists, other activists and Greens Party politicians. But most of the time, particularly towards the end of her sit, Miranda was solo. She was, however, extremely well organised and made sure she remained in touch. Armed with a solar panel and a computer, Miranda explained,

> I shared that forest with the world: blogging and speaking via video link to conferences, school groups and festivals. I was able to expose the reality of forest destruction in Tasmania, particularly important for those international customers purchasing wood products from here, many of which have been misleadingly labelled as 'eco' products despite being sourced from high conservation value forests.[21]

For the one-year anniversary she was thanked by musicians Nick Cave and John Butler, as well as former Greens Party leader Bob Brown. When she descended, Brown was there to embrace her.

Aside from a tarpaulin positioned over her sleeping bag and food area to keep them dry, Miranda lived all that time outside. For safety's sake, she always wore a harness that was strapped to the tree. It meant that even if the platform fell, she wouldn't. It's rather like the Korowai's way of treating the possible outbreak of fire: the fireplace will drop before the house catches fire. It's also a moving symbol of Miranda's relationship with the tree: she was trying to protect it while its strength protected her. She feels 'really close to the tree' and continues to visit it. Her time there had the quality of 'a personal journey'.[22] The Observer Tree is a *Eucalyptus delegatensis*, commonly known in Tasmania as Alpine Ash, a straight, grey-trunked tree which can reach heights of over 90 metres.

What were the sensations of arriving back on terra firma? Miranda maintained an exercise regime on the platform, mainly yoga and sit-ups, so her muscles wouldn't atrophy. But returning to ground level did not provide the expected relief. In fact, as Miranda tells me thoughtfully, that was 'the biggest challenge. I thought that the things I'd missed, like a warm bath, would be really important. But they weren't. I wanted to be back in the tree'. While Gibson had steeled herself as best she could for the tree-sit, she didn't have time to ready herself for coming down. When the bushfire took off it was a case of an anxious watch and wait and then, skedaddle. Once on the ground, Miranda felt she had landed in 'another world', a place she'd viewed from 60 metres up and that was 'inaccessible'. A kind of 'separation anxiety' ensued that lasted for months. She felt she'd been 'thrown overboard into the ocean, completely lost'.[23]

It's tricky to discuss intense feelings for the natural world without couching them in spiritual or transcendent terms, and Miranda is wary about describing her experience in that way. Friends suggested it sounded like she'd fallen in love with the tree and she agrees 'it does have aspects of that'. Her relationship with the tree also 'felt reciprocal ... I struggle to understand how that tree and that forest have a connection to me. That's what it feels like and I can still feel it'.[24] During the last months in the tree, the deep solitude heightened Miranda's sense of rapport with the forest.

In *The Hidden Life of Trees* Peter Wohlleben convincingly makes the case that the forest is a social network. Drawing on scientific research, he likens trees to human families: tree parents live together with their children, communicate with them, support them as they grow, share nutrients with those who are sick or struggling, and even warn each other of impending dangers. 'Can plants think?' Wohlleben asks. 'Are they intelligent?'[25]

Biologist Daniel Chamovitz believes so. In his book *What a Plant Knows*, Chamovitz outlines his research indicating that plants and animals share DNA. While Chamovitz recognises that his use of the word know is unorthodox—plants don't have a central nervous system, a brain that coordinates information for the entire body as we do—nonetheless 'plants monitor their visible environment all the time. Plants see you if you come near them: they know when you stand over them. They even know if you're wearing a blue or a red shirt'.[26]

Of course, plants don't see as we do: but they do apprehend light in many ways and colours that we can only imagine. For example, plants see the same ultraviolet light that gives us sunburn and infrared light that heats us up. In some cases, the plant kingdom can reveal itself as sentient and smart. Intelligence is as important for evolutionary survival for plants as it is for animals, including us. But Chamovitz is frankly dismissive of 'the myriad gardeners and plant biologists who develop what they consider to be personal relationships with their plants'. He regards such relationships as 'not dissimilar' to that between a child and her imaginary friend.[27]

If Miranda fell in love with the tree, did the tree fall in love with Miranda? It seems like the stuff of fairy tales, resembling the Ents, the walking, talking tree-like creatures in JRR Tolkien's *The Lord of the Rings*. But, taking Chamovitz's cue, was The Observer Tree aware Miranda had parked herself in its canopy, as did other members of the ecosystem, for example, the Currawongs? Though the Observer Tree could not see Miranda like the Currawongs did, was it able to register her presence? What did the tree 'think' of her? She was there a hell of a long time, so it probably got used to this unusual visitor. Quite a rarity at that height. The tree had its own forest family to take care of and it was getting on with the business of growing and surviving.

If we share DNA with plants, what else can we share? Did the tree feel it protected the little human animal in its branches? Did it wish Miranda well? Perhaps one day we will be able to chart the reciprocity that Miranda sensed, not as a poetic flight of fantasy or a human palimpsest on the natural world, but as data borne out by scientific evidence, a precise and more encompassing version of feeling 'at one' with nature—an experience with which we're all familiar, even if it lasts only a few moments.

It often strikes me as curious that we need to minutely inter-rogate our relationship with the natural world, when First Nations people, on whose mythologies so many cultures have been built and enriched, have no issue whatsoever with finding a spiritual (and practical) bridge between the human/animal/plant zones. For them, an ecosystem is a lived reality. I have no doubt the Korowai would appreciate Miranda's courage and tenacity as well as under-standing her intimacy with the forest, an intimacy they share. Our (civilised) distrust of nature is a factor which hampers our protection of the natural world, as if we (humans) will always know best when it comes to governing and aiding that world. Anthropomorphism strikes me as a lack of imagination and generosity.

Miranda's resolve was born from a previous protest. She was part of Tasmania's longest running forest blockade in the Florentine Valley, which began in 2006. The protest stopped much of the logging and won World Heritage protection for most of that land. Miranda's Observer Tree–sit was successful, too. In 2013, Tasmania's Wilderness World Heritage Area was officially extended by 170 000 hectares, and that included the Tyenna Valley. It's a listing which remains in place.

GARDENS
OF EDEN

O N A SULTRY summer afternoon in 2002, I caught the tube to Hampstead to visit the Freud Museum London. I was taking a break after the publication of *Australian Gothic: a Life of Albert Tucker*. Writing some books can wring the life out of you, and that one did for me. Though I had Bert's approval and worked closely with him, he decided to wait until I'd finished the manuscript before he read it. So when Bert died in 1999, he hadn't read a word.

When his widow Barbara read the manuscript, it seemed she took umbrage at my suggestion that Joy Hester, his first wife, played an influential role in his creative development and that the rupture of their marriage in 1947 was a wound that never quite healed for him. I say seemed because Barbara denied that was the problem. She kept insisting there were 'factual errors' in the manuscript. What were they? How could I fix them? She'd already suggested forty changes to the text and I'd made them all. The whole manuscript must be rewritten. But how and why? She refused to say.

Barbara then set about doing everything she could to stop the book being published.

All through 2001, and incessantly, Jane Palfreyman, my publisher at Random House Australia, and I dealt with lawyers and, once the stoush became public, journalists. The matter made the papers and the evening news. The situation grew even more complicated when the board of Heide Museum of Modern Art, of which I was a member, decided I should resign. Barbara was in the process of donating a sizeable bequest to Heide, which included works by Tucker, Hester, Arthur Boyd and other major artists. The board opined there was a conflict of interest. I refused to comply. I attended a board meeting where every member, including those who had previously supported me, turned on me, and gave me hell. I walked out to find an ABC film crew waiting in the foyer for an interview. Later I watched myself on TV at a friend's place. All I remember is the sight of me walking away. While I received moving support from many in the arts and beyond, around the country, I was often fretful, and anxious about what might happen next.

Australian Gothic finally went ahead, though without Bert's paintings because Barbara owned the copyright and she denied permission to reproduce them. Fortunately, Bert's moving and evocative photographs were exempt and so we illustrated the book with them. *Australian Gothic* received a hearteningly positive response but I was a nervous wreck. I needed to fly to another shore, immerse myself in another culture, have my imagination freshly piqued.

I stayed at Goodenough College in Mecklenburgh Square, a residential wing of London University that was available to travelling scholars. It's in Bloomsbury. Fittingly, Virginia and Leonard Woolf had lived in an apartment on the same site until 1940 when they were bombed out during the Blitz. The Woolfs settled in Sussex. (I'll take you there a little later). Goodenough College was a graceful and pleasant place and my room was small, light-filled and modern. From my window I could see the enclosed garden at the square's heart for which I was given a key. I felt rather like a child in a fairy tale entering the garden, yet also slightly discomfited, in my democratic Australian way, that I should have access to this treasure while others didn't. In fact, Goodenough College was rather beyond my budget. Being a full-time writer rarely gives you enough money for luxuries, making them all the more delicious and necessary.

I knew that Freud had a collection of antiquities but I had no idea of its quality or scope. My knowledge of Freud was slight. I'd been impressed by *The Interpretation of Dreams* (1899) and his essay 'Mourning and Melancholia' (1917) but I knew nothing about the man's life, who he was, what made him tick.

I got lost on the way to the museum, had to backtrack and change trains, and I wondered if it was a Freudian slip. Did I really want to visit Freud's home? Was there some form of resistance going on? Emerging from the station at Finchley Road, a roaring, brutally ugly thoroughfare, I spotted a small sign indicating the route to the museum. I was rather disappointed, having imagined Hampstead festooned with posters of Freud, the stern-faced, white-bearded, implacable father of the sexual revolution.

Freud had arrived in London in 1938, when the Nazi invasion of Vienna had forced him to flee. It was a terrible journey. Freud was eighty-three and suffering from cancer of the upper palate. He'd had to abandon his home of forty years at Berggasse 19, Vienna, now the Sigmund Freud Museum. There was also the chance that his collection of 2500 antiquities may not arrive, even though Freud had won clearance for it from the Nazi authorities. 'The gangsters are unpredictable,' Freud observed.[1] After buying a house at 20 Maresfield Gardens, he settled in with his wife Martha, Minna Bernays, his sister-in-law, and Anna, his youngest daughter, a pioneering psychoanalyst of children. In August 1938, to Freud's relief, the antiquities were delivered. Miraculously, nothing was missing or broken.

Maresfield Gardens is an ordinary, tree-lined, middle-class street. Freud's home is spacious and comfortable, its status so discreetly advertised it's easy to miss. After paying the admission fee, I wandered into Freud's study where I stopped, dazzled, captivated.

In the fusty-smelling room, the daylight excluded by velvet drapes, I was surrounded by an array of small, exquisite, ancient objects crowded on every surface, an intriguing catalogue of world civilisations where objects rare and sacred, useful and arcane, ravaged and lovely were on view: Neolithic tools, delicate Sumerian

seals, a great goddess of the Middle Bronze Age, Egyptian mummy
bandages inscribed with magical spells and stained with embalming
ointment, superb Hellenistic statues, images of the Sphinx, erotic
Roman charms and Chinese jade lions no bigger than a baby's
fist. Commanding attention was Freud's couch, the icon of
psychoanalysis, arguably the most famous piece of furniture in the
world, adorned with a richly coloured, finely woven Persian rug.

I don't know how long I was there. The minutes slipped away.
Several times I walked to the front door, then turned around
and went back to the study. It was like Luis Buñuel's film *The
Exterminating Angel* where the characters try to leave a house but,
on reaching the threshold, feel inexplicably compelled to stay.

Sigmund Freud's couch, © Freud Museum London.

There was a kindly fellow at the front desk. I was there so long, I think he'd begun to suspect I was going to nick something. He took a photo of me standing in the midst of the collection. I was smiling, radiant.

My mind was brimming with questions. How did Freud afford this? How long did it take to amass? Why choose antiquities and not modern art? Most importantly, why wasn't the collection better known? Sigmund Freud may have prescribed therapy for his patients, while his personal preference was for retail therapy. Freud was a shopaholic and an obsessive art collector. It prompted me to write a book—*The Gods of Freud: Sigmund Freud's art collection* (2006).

It now strikes me as curious, amusing and fortuitous, that hurting with psychological wounds after the stoush over *Australian Gothic*, I found myself in a place of healing belonging to one of the leading 'healers' of the modern era. A place in which I felt compelled to stay. I'm sure Freud, who was devoted to coincidence, symbolism and 'Freudian slips', would have approved and indeed welcomed me to remain, find succour and learn. Also, Freud was tremendously proud of the collection and was disappointed by the lack of interest shown by his patients and colleagues. I was going to make it up to him. I'd do everything I could to see that the collection was better known, including bringing an exhibition to Australia.

After gaining the approval of the museum's director, there were regular trips back to London to work on the collection which continued up until 2014. I would climb behind the burgundy ropes, which kept back visitors, to sit, cross-legged on the floor near Freud's desk, making notes and taking photos of works. Or simply contemplating the collection: its visual impact, the arrangement of objects, Freud's curation of his beloved treasures. The freedom I was given was wonderful and I remain extremely grateful that the staff accorded me such an honour.

I never did get to lie on the couch—I've heard tell that sometimes an esteemed visitor is granted this privilege. The couch, the seductive symbol of psychoanalysis, of dreams, fantasies and memories, was given to him in 1891 by a grateful patient. It is a well-padded chaise longue, on which a patient could stretch at full length. Freud decorated it with an exquisite Persian rug, transforming the solid, plain and rather ugly sofa into a deliciously comfortable object, glowing with patterns and textures, which took pride of place in his rooms. Not only did Freud cover the couch with a rug but he attached another to the wall next to it, creating a cocoon effect. Freud placed light wool rugs nearby, surrounding the patient with warmth and luxury. Freud, meanwhile, settled himself in a moss-green velvet chair that was accompanied by a foot stool, and puffed on his interminable cigars.

Freud chose a Qashqai rug, woven by the women of a nomadic tribe from southern Iran. They are among the most admired of Persian carpets. At the time Freud bought his, the Qashqai were producing rugs 'so fine it is difficult to believe they were made by human hand'.[2] The rug depicts a garden. Its deep, warm tones of madder red and ochre, and its intricate geometric patterns, represent the cultural continuity of a proud, independent minority group. Qashqai men are expert horsemen and herders; the women are renowned for their weaving and their brilliantly coloured clothes.

Today many Qashqai have settled in towns, though some continue the tough, time-honoured, nomadic life. Their annual pilgrimages take them from the warmer zone of the Persian Gulf, where they winter with their herds, to the cooler regions of the Zagros Mountains for the summer, a journey of about 500 kilometres. Most rugs are not made to sell. They are an important dowry item and the weaver's skill is esteemed. Each rug is made of silky, lustrous wool from the tribe's sheep herds. Each is unique and takes months to make. The weavers gather herbs, barks and berries to boil in a collective dyebath. They rarely consult patterns or designs: the rugs are artworks, a form of self-expression.

Freud's rug, festooned with abstracted trees, flowers and birds, depicts a Paradise garden, a mythical Eden. Paradise comes from *pairi-daeza*, which is Avestan for walled enclosure, while Eden is related to the Aramaic root word 'fruitful, well-watered', inferring an ordered, irrigated garden in a dry land, a blissful and aesthetically pleasing refuge. The rug's geometric patterns 'enclose' the trees and flowers in the same way a garden is organised with borders, paths and fences. 'This vision of Paradise, this dream of a richly watered garden, of superabundant nature'[3] is typical of the nomad rug for, in the arid Middle East, 'gardens are so precious as to be truly paradise'.[4] The Qashqai weavers, nomads without gardens, travelling through harsh, dry country, created images of desire, ideals of fecundity and pleasure.

The Arabian Nights, first written in Persian and later translated into Arabic, is set in a walled garden where Scheherazade beguiled the emperor with her tales. Betrayed by his wife, whom he'd had beheaded, the emperor threatened to avenge his honour by executing another woman each dawn. For a thousand and one nights, Scheherazade's stories of flying carpets, genies and treasure-filled caves enchanted the emperor and deflected him from his purpose. On a rug created by women, Freud's patients, who were mostly women, captivated him with their tales, woven from the fabric of their dreams and memories.

The word oasis conjures an image of cool, blessed relief for the nomad and the desert traveller. The precious fruitful places, created by the emergence of underground water, are often shaded by tall Date Palms which help humans, animals and other plants to survive.

The Date Palm (*Phoenix dactylifera L.*) has a long and illustrious history. While the first evidence of its cultivation was in southern Mesopotamia around 5000 BC, oasis agriculture seems to have developed mainly from around 3000 BC when it appeared in different parts of the Middle East: Mesopotamia, Iran and eastern Arabia.[5] 'Does any of you wish that he should have a garden with date-palms and vines and streams flowing underneath, and all kinds of fruit?' asks the Koran. The fruit from the Date Palm is deliciously sweet—dried it will keep for months—while the tree's extraordinary lushness and hardiness have given it a major symbolic function in Greek and Roman cultures, as well as Judaism and Christianity.

Date Palms at an oasis, Um El Ma, Sahara Desert, Libya, KarlHeinz Irlmeier. imageBROKER/ Alamy Stock Photo, 2004.

You might be surprised to learn that Freud was a forest fancier and delved deeply into the natural world. An ardent amateur botanist, he was always on the hunt for rare plants and flower specimens. He was an expert on varieties of trees and even enjoyed eating them, a habit begun in childhood. Admitting it was a somewhat odd request, Freud asked his friend Eduard Silberstein to locate a type of Cypress because its twigs and needles were delicious, but 'you have to be a seasoned eater of leaves and branches like myself to detect it'.[6]

Freud built the entire edifice of psychoanalysis on childhood memories. By the age of three the compass was set. When it came to telling the story of his own childhood, Freud created a fairy tale.

Once upon a time, he played in the forest near the small town of Freiberg in Moravia, then part of Austria–Hungary and now Příbor, Czech Republic. He had been born there in 1856. Freud loved the forest and escaped from his father to lose himself in its depths. Freiberg is ringed by the magnificent snow-capped

Beskydy Mountains, part of the Carpathians, which stretch across Central and Eastern Europe for over 1500 kilometres.

When Freud was three, this idyllic existence ended. Freud explained, 'the branch of the industry [textiles] in which my father was concerned met with a catastrophe. He lost all his means and we were forced to leave'.[7] The family moved first to Leipzig, then to Vienna. Freud drew a veil across that time. As far as he was concerned, the long and difficult years that followed were simply not worth remembering. Leaving Freiberg was such a shock, it gave Freud a kind of amnesia and there were gaps when he tried to recall his early years in Vienna. 'I never really felt comfortable' in Vienna, Freud complained, and ached for 'the beautiful woods near my home'.[8]

While researching my book on Freud, I made my way to Příbor and found Freud's forest. It remains a bewitching place, a vivid contrast of sunlight and shadow, rivered with paths, where copses of Silver Birch give way to the engulfing dark of the Pines. The ground is covered with a tangle of grasses, wildflowers and thick pine needles. The air is alive with birdsong. It's a wonderful place for a child to play. Less than 2 kilometres from the town, Jacob Freud could have carried his small son there.

Freud addressed his paradise lost by spending long summer holidays in forests. As his family of six grew, he organised vacations at a variety of spectacular mountain retreats in Austria and Italy's South Tyrol. Going to the mountains with his brood was 'the greatest fun' for Freud.[9] In the Dolomites, Martha, Freud's wife, and Minna, her sister, went strolling together: anything more vigorous tired them. But Freud's daughter Anna adored travelling with Freud, and their mountain vacations gave Anna the chance to set off alone on hikes with her father. Holidays were precious to the Freud children because it provided them with their annual allotment of their father's attention. The rest of the time, Freud was busy seeing patients and writing the sexual history of Western civilisation. Freud was a delightful and informative guide on such excursions, taking his children on mushroom hunts and rambles through 'wild forests and woods' where he would describe butterflies, flowers and anything else that caught his fancy.[10]

Living so close to Hampstead Heath proved a treat for Anna, as it does for anyone who visits that vast, verdant treasure in the middle of one of the world's most hectic cities. (A word of warning: if you plan to visit the Heath, don't go on a weekend when it becomes as frantic as the rest of London.) Manorial rights to the land remained in private hands until the 1940s when they lapsed under Sir Spencer Pocklington Maryon-Wilson, and gradually it became common land, and part of the City of London.

Hampstead Heath, London, Janine Burke, 2014.

When you walk through the groves of massive Oak and Plane trees, and cross the spacious fields, the pleasure and recreation the Heath has offered people over the years is palpable. The Heath feels treasured. In her declining years, Anna sought refuge there, too. Wrapped in her father's coat, she was taken by wheel chair to the Heath. Perhaps it recalled happy times spent roaming through forests with her father.

In the Judaic–Christian tradition, a garden is where humanity began. Most poignantly, Eden's symbolic power resides in a sense of loss, when Eve, seduced by the sophistry of a serpent, ate a forbidden fruit, leading to banishment. A narrative that probably originated as a folk tale has had, as Pamela Norris writes, 'an unprecedented influence on how Western society has defined its moral and spiritual identity'.[11] Central to the story is a tree.

In Genesis, God instructs Adam to maintain and cherish the garden, 'to till it … and keep it'. Adam could also feast on the fruits of the trees, except for one that was in the middle of the garden— the tree of the knowledge of good and evil. God warned, 'you may not take [it]; for on the day when you take of it, death will certainly come to you'. It seems that Eve, created shortly afterwards by God from Adam's rib, was intrigued by the tree. She was loitering nearby when a serpent struck up a conversation with her. Perhaps all the animals in Paradise could talk: Eve wasn't surprised by a chatty snake. The serpent convinced Eve that, by eating the fruit, not only would she escape death, she would herself become a god. Gazing at the tree, Eve 'saw that it was good for food, and a delight to the eyes, and to be desired to make one wise'. So she plucked a fruit and took a bite—presumably it was delicious—and shared it with Adam.

Though Genesis does not identify the tree, it has been traditionally regarded as an Apple, making it the fruit of temptation and consolidating its reputation from Classical times as a symbol of fecundity. Artists revelled in the sexy, dramatic scene which cast comely Eve/Woman as a temptress whose wiles the hapless Adam/Man was unable to withstand. Lucas Cranach the Elder couldn't leave the story alone and painted several versions. In *Adam and Eve,* (1526, Courtauld Institute Galleries, London), the couple stand on either side of the tree. Bemused, Adam scratches his head while Eve, a saucy minx with a pale, curvaceous body and long, golden hair, smirks as she proffers him the apple.

Eden is a peaceable kingdom. Animals surround the couple. A boar grazes on the grass like a cow. As any sixteenth-century hunter knew, a boar was a fierce creature that, if cornered, could tear a man apart. A shaggy lion lies near the boar, docile as the family dog. Near Adam's feet rests a stag with magnificent antlers, its horns perilously close to Adam's genitals, which are discreetly covered with vine leaves. The tree's boughs are laden with large, rosy apples. Behind the tree stand other cultivated trees: Paradise is an orchard.

The scenes that follow are tragi-comic. Strolling through the garden that evening, God realises that Adam and Eve are hiding from him. The fruit has delivered its sting: Adam and Eve recognise themselves as sexual beings and they are embarrassed by their nakedness. Like an angry parent, God interrogates them and they, like children caught red-handed, play the blame game—Adam accusing Eve, and Eve the snake. Then they're expelled from Eden while an angel with a fiery sword protects a second important tree—the tree of life, of immortality. God isn't prepared to countenance the threat of more disobedience from his far too independently minded humans in case they pilfer that tree and rival him in eternity. Though God cursed Eve, she is, in Cranach's eyes, a goddess—as luscious, commanding and impetuous as Venus, another femme fatale whom Cranach often painted.

While the 'site' of the Garden of Eden is unknown, it's not entirely in the land of myth. There are clues, which don't quite add up, to rivers such as the Tigris and the Euphrates, which form a delta with the river that flows through Paradise. Somewhere near Babylon? Ethiopia, perhaps?

But, unlike Eden, it is known where the domestic apple originated. In Central Asia, in the Tien Shan, or Celestial Mountains, of Kazakhstan to be precise. The original wild fruit forests of *Malus sieversii*, which became *Malus domestica*, are growing there today. *Malus sieversii* evolved in China about twelve million years ago and its seeds were carried by birds to Tien Shan and the valley of the Ili River, where the apple found itself, as Roger Deakin writes, 'in a genuine paradise'.[12] Bears lived in the woodlands—the Tien Shan White-Clawed Bear—and they selected the sweeter, juicier apples while bees laboured in the pollination department of the

Wild Apple Groves, Tien Shan Mountains, Kazakhstan.

same evolutionary project. Bear claws are expertly adapted to grasp fruit, of which they are avid consumers. From the early Bronze Age, around 2000 BC, humans and horses helped, too, as they plied the great trade routes from China to the Danube, carrying apples in saddlebags, eating them, then defecating the seeds and spreading them far and wide.

Discovering the apple's origin was no mean feat, as Barrie Juniper of Oxford University's Department of Plant Sciences can attest.[13] In 1998, Juniper, together with several Oxford colleagues, travelled to Almaty, the 'City of Apples', in Kazakhstan. The apple is the world's main fruit crop in temperate regions and Juniper wished to map its genetic identity through DNA samples. It had taken Juniper a year of negotiating with Kazakh officials to visit the remote Tien Shan area but eventually, in the summer of 1998, under military escort, Juniper set out from Almaty. There in the Celestial Mountains, he found the forests of wild fruit, not only of apples but of pears, plums and apricots, thriving in the thin, clean air. Juniper's analysis was confirmed when the complete genome of the apple was decoded in 2010. An international team of scientists, including horticultural genomicists from Washington State University, proved *Malus sieversii* was the domestic apple's wild ancestor.

However, the tree of knowledge of good and evil was not an Apple. Apples weren't cultivated in that part of the world in biblical times. Some suggest it may have been a Pomegranate or a Quince. But eating a pomegranate is messy: it requires splitting open the tough skin, then using fingers or a spoon to retrieve the translucent, ruby-red seeds. Could Eve have been bothered even if there were spoons in Paradise? Quinces are an ancient fruit: the Persians cultivated them and also used their perfume as a breath freshener. But neither fruit has the romance of the apple which remains a powerful image of fecundity.

In 1976, when Steve Jobs and Steve Wozniak founded Apple Inc., the American multinational computer company, the logo they chose was an apple with one bite taken out—a triumph for Eve in the popular imagination.

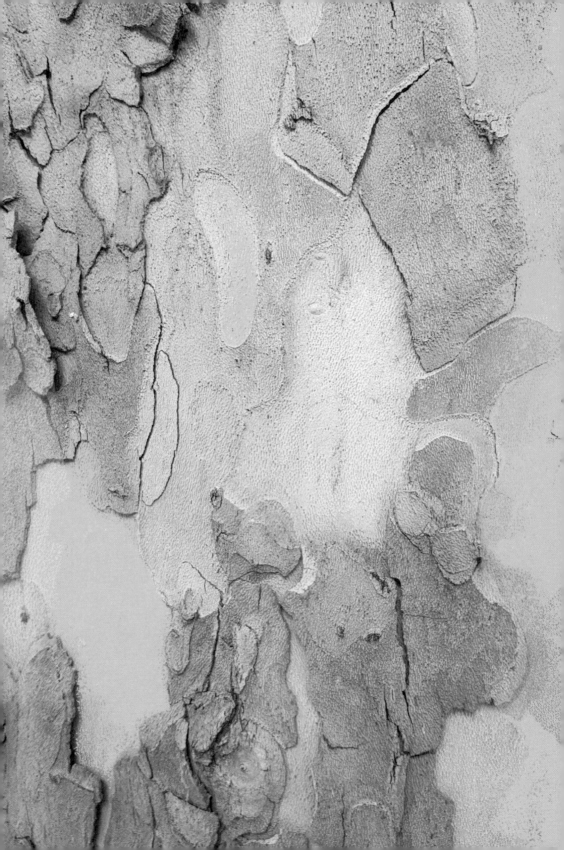

TREES
OF JESUS

Though I'm here in my study, reading the Bible for this chapter, I must confess I'm not a Christian. Perhaps being educated in Catholic girls' schools and taught by a series of grumpy nuns unqualified as teachers rather alienated me. As a ten-year-old confessing my sins to the shadowy figure of a priest seated behind a curtain in the confessional, it seemed I had nothing very startling to report. Really nothing to report at all, unless squabbling with my sister about who would have first shower in the morning counted. Well, yes, it did. Three Our Fathers and six Hail Marys were tallied as my punishment.

But one must admire Jesus, a rare being radiant with self-confidence and radical attitudes towards the wealthy and the hypocrites of this world, as well as to the poor and the forsaken. Goodness knows what he would make of the Catholic Church today, with its deplorable history of child sexual abuse and its fantastic riches and power.

Jesus's biography could be written in terms of trees. He inter-acted with them from his birth to his death, making trees stand like sentinels at each major chapter of his life. At his birth, a group of mysterious visitors brought precious scented resins as an offering. Later, Jesus became a woodworker, a carpenter, trained by Joseph, his father. On Palm Sunday, his preaching and miracle-working now legendary, he made a triumphant entry into Jerusalem, hailed by his followers waving palm fronds.

Four days later, Jesus suffered torments of the mind in Gethsemane, an Olive grove, where he awaited his fate. His torture at the behest of Pontius Pilate, the Roman governor, saw him decked with a crown of thorns and then forced to carry, before being nailed to, a wooden cross. Much later, in popular culture, the birth of Jesus came to be celebrated with a Pine tree, a sentimental favourite decked with ornaments and surrounded by presents. Jesus is also part of a religious tradition centred on a dying and resurrecting tree god from Greek mythology.

Who were 'the wise men from the East', or magi, and why did they offer the Christ child the perfumed resin of certain trees? It's only in the Gospel of Matthew the visitors are mentioned. They arrive in Jerusalem and unnerve King Herod by asking, 'Where is he that is born King of the Jews? for we have seen his star in the east, and are come to worship him.' This came as no surprise to the local priests who advised Herod that 'it was written by the prophet' that in Bethlehem 'a Governor' will be born 'that shall rule my people Israel'. Herod, anxious about being usurped, suggested the magi continue on to Bethlehem, find the child and bring him back to the court. It was a ruse, of course, to murder the little one.

As the magi set off, they were delighted to see the star that had guided them rise above the place where Joseph, Mary and Jesus were staying. Upon arriving, they 'fell down and worshipped him. When they had opened their treasures, they presented unto him gifts: gold, and frankincense, and myrrh.' As Ed Cumming notes, they are the most famous Christmas presents in history.[1] A series of dreams then protected both the family and the magi from catastrophe: the magi dreamed they should not return home via Jerusalem, while Joseph was instructed by a dream angel to flee with Mary and Jesus to Egypt. A lucky escape because after Herod realised he'd been tricked by the magi, he ordered the slaughter of all male children in Bethlehem under the age of two. It's worth noting there's no historical proof for any of these events.

Among the earliest representations of the magi appears in 526 AD in the glowing mosaics of the Basilica of Sant'Apollinare Nuovo in Ravenna, Italy. The mosaic depicts three men with their names—Balthassar, Melchior and Gaspar—displayed above their heads, though Matthew cited neither their number nor their names. The trio's strong, rhythmic, forward movement with gifts in hand and cloaks billowing makes it seem they are making a dash towards the still, commanding central figures of Mary and her child. The magi's costumes are Phrygian as are their caps, indicating it was thought that their home was Persia (part of modern-day Iran). If so,

Basilica of Sant'Apollinare Nuovo, Ravenna, 526 AD, Emme Pi Travel/Alamy Stock Photo, 2008.

that was quite a journey. In the magi's time, it would have meant
months of hard slog across the desert with a caravanserai of servants
and camels.

By the early Renaissance, the event had become something of
a party as the resplendent detail of Gentile da Fabriano's *Adoration
of the Magi* (1423, Uffizi, Florence) shows. Haloes—an indicator
of holiness and/or sainthood—adorn the magi. Their clothes are
richly embroidered and they hold elegant golden canisters containing their gifts. Surrounding them is a crowded retinue of men and
horses. Gaspar, represented as an elderly gentleman, is on his knees,
leaning forward to kiss the feet of the Christ child. The *Adoration
of the Magi*, or the Epiphany (in Greek, *epiphaneia*, meaning literally
appearance, manifestation) as it's known in Western Christianity, is
celebrated on 6 January, two weeks after the birth of Jesus.

Adoration of the Magi, (detail), 1423, Gentile da Fabriano, tempera on panel, 300 × 282 cm,
The Uffizi, Florence, Heritage Image Partnership Ltd/Alamy Stock Photo.

The term 'magi' is derived from the Greek *magos*, which in turn was derived from the Persian term for the astronomer-priests of the Zoroastrian religion. An early monotheistic faith, Zoroastrianism is named after its prophet Zoroaster or Zarathustra, and it was Persia's official religion in Jesus's time. The magi were highly regarded astrologers. In that era, the science of astronomy and the arts of astrology were interchangeable. The magi read the heavens in order to give advice and solace to their followers, especially those of royal ilk. By connecting the magi to the guiding star, Matthew was sending a message to the readers of the Gospels that not only did knowledgeable and esteemed priests identify baby Jesus as the Son of God, but their visit validated the prophecy.

What prompted their selection of gifts? Gold is a present anyone would welcome and it must have been quite overwhelming for Mary and Joseph to have such wealth unexpectedly placed in their hands. In Gentile da Fabriano's painting, as in many representations of the Epiphany, the family is depicted as residing in the stable where Jesus was born, underscoring their poverty. Poor Mary. Imagine giving birth in a stable with no midwife save Joseph, and surrounded by critters that include a donkey plus cows and sheep. The place would have stunk to high heaven. (That's the last pun. I promise.)

Frankincense and myrrh? Those resins were considered so valuable that they then cost roughly the same as gold. Frankincense, in particular, was big business. Ancient Egyptians used it as an aid to embalming corpses, while it was also an ingredient in kohl, a dramatic black eyeliner worn by women, which remains popular to this day. Jews, Muslims and Christians used it in a variety of religious and cultural events, while the Romans, who adored baths—constructing them everywhere possible in the empire— scented the water with this resin.

Frankincense was traded on the Arabian Peninsula and the Horn of Africa and all through the Negev Desert for more than five thousand years, along what came to be known as the Incense Road. Travel on the route was arduous but there were plenty of oases, stationed about 40 kilometres apart, places to meet with other travellers, swap stories, water, feed and rest themselves, their retinue and their animals. Even do a little shopping. We learn from the Bible that the fabled Queen of Sheba travelled the road when she visited Jerusalem to seek King Solomon's wisdom. She was laden with gifts, including 'gold, large quantities of spices, and precious stones'. For spices, read frankincense and myrrh. Basically, the queen was on a trade mission.

But the magi's purpose was different: they were on a sacred quest dictated by a magical star which showed them where a powerful spiritual leader had been born. They paid homage with the same treasures that the Queen of Sheba brought to Solomon: gifts worthy of a king. No doubt it was merely a legend, something Matthew concocted for dramatic historic effect, evidence of divine fatalism, the fruition of prophecy. But I do hope, for the sake of Joseph and Mary's finances, that they did indeed receive those gifts and it helped their scramble for existence.

The sacred significance of frankincense in ritual is mentioned frequently in the Bible. From Exodus 30:34,

And the Lord said unto Moses, Take unto thee sweet spices … ; these sweet spices with pure frankincense: of each shall there be a like weight:
      And thou shalt make it a perfume, a confection after the art of the apothecary, tempered together, pure and holy:
And thou shalt beat some of it very small, and put of it before the testimony in the tabernacle of the congregation, where I will meet with thee: it shall be unto you most holy.
And as for the perfume which thou shalt make, ye shall not make to yourselves according to the composition thereof: it shall be unto thee holy for the Lord.

Frankincense (Middle English: *franke ensens* from Old French *franc encens*, pure incense) is tapped from scraggy, hardy trees (Boswellia) by slashing the bark and allowing the exuded resin to bleed out and harden. The hardened resins are called, poetically, tears. Boswellia has an unusual and useful ability to flourish in environments so unforgiving that sometimes the trees grow out of solid rock. The trees start producing resin when they are about eight to ten years old. Tapping is done two to three times a year, with the final taps producing the best tears due to their higher aromatic content. Generally speaking, the more opaque the resins, the better the quality. It's expensive because it's difficult to cultivate.

I first became acquainted with frankincense and myrrh as a child. Benediction was an entertaining church ceremony. It offered what the Catholic Church can do so spectacularly well: theatre. A priest in sumptuous, gold-embroidered robes placed the resins in a shining brass canister swung rhythmically to spread the fragrance throughout the church. The congregation sang melodious Latin chants of whose meaning I knew nothing. Plus, it was all over in twenty minutes.

So, in a spirit of reverie and research, I'm at this moment burning frankincense. I've taken a small, four-legged, brass bowl and sat it on a jade coaster on my desk. Then I sprinkled its base with salt and placed on top a circular piece of charcoal (from a company, incidentally, named Three Kings), which I lit. As the charcoal burned and began to turn ashen, I carefully arranged tiny pieces of frankincense on it. They look like dark gold nuggets. Now my study is filled with heady, sweet-smelling smoke. Quite a lot of smoke, actually. It's burning like crazy and the bowl is hot to the touch.

The frankincense I purchased from Miriam, the Voodoo Queen of New Orleans, in her shop near Congo Square, crammed with feathers, books, photographs and precious stones. (We'll revisit New Orleans.) The incense wasn't expensive, so perhaps it's not of a high standard, though it certainly smells divine. Frankincense's popularity in ancient times was not only because of its perfume. It was believed to have spiritually cleansing properties, getting rid of pesky evil spirits, bad vibes and suchlike. I must say my mind has become rather perkier, as I'd been experiencing a mild, mid-afternoon slump. As long as the smoke alarm doesn't go off. The word perfume derives from the French *parfum*, from *parfumer*, to scent; from *par* + *fumer*, smoke. Merely watching it burn is mesmerising: the vapours arching and looping as they weave in the air.

The story of the magi has certainly not helped the survival of Boswellia. Quite the reverse. There's been a reignition of interest in the symbolic and perfume properties of the tree. That's due to a global market for essential oils, the demands of the cosmetics market together with a revival of pagan rituals. There was also a bizarre and dangerous theory doing the rounds on the internet that frankincense may be a cure for cancer. It's put Boswellia in danger of extinction.

Today the bulk of the world's frankincense is sourced from wild populations of Boswellia found in the Horn of Africa, especially Ethiopia. Recent research led by ecologist Frans Bongers of Wageningen University and Research in the Netherlands reveals the trees cannot cope with the number of times they are being tapped for commercial purposes.[2] Though the farmers make more money, in the process they are killing the trees. The pressure, of course, is poverty.

While the trees are found in rugged, mountainous regions, the loss of forests is gradually destroying Ethiopia's remaining woodlands. That's due to the rapid increase in human population together with the expansion of cattle and goat herds. Ethiopia is Africa's second largest nation, with a population of around 101 million.

The future looks grim for frankincense. There are few young trees in the forests while the older ones are exhausted. Bongers's research indicates the collapse of Boswellia's numbers: frankincense production could be halved in the next twenty years. There's a

Harvesting the resin of a Frankincense Tree near Mughsayl, Dhofar Region, Oman, image/ BROKER Fabian von Poser/Alamy Stock Photo, 2014.

small hope that due to the demand from the perfume industry— for example, frankincense is an ingredient for major perfume producers like Chanel and Guerlain—customers may insist on ethically and sustainably sourced materials. The chain of command regarding trade and profit favours those who own the land where the trees are found. The local people who harvest the resin don't own the property and thus receive the least amount of cash, while the suppliers for the religious and cosmetic markets profit.

Matthew and Mark tell us that Jesus was a carpenter. One day Jesus had been preaching in the temple and offending the priests, as usual. The priests ask, 'Is this not the carpenter's son? Is not his mother called Mary?' The words are similar in both Matthew 13:55 and Mark 6:3. The priests' reaction can be summarised as,

'Who does this guy think he is!?!' It also implies the carpenter's trade was regarded as menial, at least in the eyes of the priests.

Joseph has always seemed something of a loser to me. The statues of him in the churches I visited as a child show a drab fellow, dressed in brown, looking rather downcast, whereas a statue of Mary, usually nearby and occupying her own chapel, traditionally depicts her as the majestic queen of heaven with a flaming golden halo, floating on a cloud and clad in fluttering and flattering blue and white robes. It was a no-brainer who I was going to pray to.

But one must feel for Joseph. His fiancee becomes pregnant, through (apparently) no action of his own. Then she is visited by an angel who tells her that she is 'with' the Son of God. In another dream (Freud would have had a field day with Joseph), Joseph is advised to stay mum about the truth of the pregnancy and to marry Mary anyway. Gallantly, Joseph does so, and without demur. If Mary is a fugitive figure in the Gospels, Joseph is practically invisible. Yet he provided guidance for his son's career, and trained him as a carpenter, starting at around twelve, the same age that Joseph would have begun his training, probably with his father. It would have been difficult to get Jesus to obey anyone, he was so clearly set on his own path. But Joseph managed. What were their trees?

John Everett Millais, a member of the Pre-Raphaelite Brotherhood, offers a detailed picture of a carpenter's workshop in the first decade AD. *Christ in the House of His Parents* (1849–50, Tate Britain, London) aroused controversy when it was exhibited. In fact, the furore was so great it put the Pre-Raphaelite Brotherhood, a relatively obscure group of young artists, on the map. Millais had co-founded the brotherhood with William Holman Holt and Dante Gabriel Rossetti in 1848, before welcoming other members to the fold. I don't know who wrote the pithy account of *Christ in the House of His Parents* in Wikipedia with its useful online references, but I'm grateful. It goes to show that Wiki, in some cases at least, has come a long way.

Viewing this sentimental, symbol-laden painting from today's standpoint, it's difficult to understand the outrage that greeted

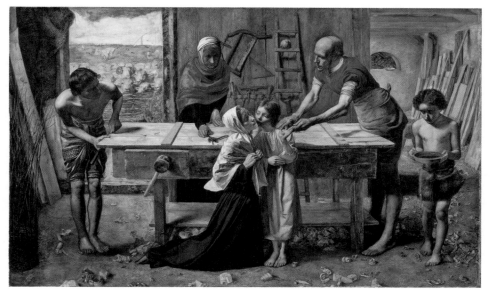

Christ in the House of His Parents ('The Carpenter's Shop'), 1849–50, John Everett Millais, oil on canvas, 86.4 × 139.7 cm, Tate Gallery Britain, Purchased with assistance from the Art Fund and various subscribers 1921, © Tate Gallery.

its exhibition. Charles Dickens went berserk. He accused Millais of portraying Mary as an alcoholic who was 'so hideous in her ugliness … that she would stand from the rest of the company as a Monster, in the vilest cabaret in France, or the lowest ginshop in England' while Jesus was a 'wry-necked, blubbering, red-headed boy, in a bed-gown'.[3] Queen Victoria was so concerned she had the painting sent to her at Buckingham Palace for a private view.

Perhaps what riled Millais's audience was that he did not glorify the family. While *Christ in the House of His Parents* might seem overly sweet to contemporary taste, in the mid-nineteenth century, such a prosaic view of Jesus and his family was scandalous. The painting is not set in Christ's home but in Joseph's workshop, where the extended family—including grandmother Anne and a juvenile John the Baptist wearing a fetching, camel hair miniskirt—is gathered. Millais, an artist at work in his own studio, presents the practical reality of Joseph's skill and labour.

The painting's narrative is that Jesus, the focus of all gazes, has cut his left palm on a nail, prefiguring his fate of being nailed to the cross. In a tender touch, Mary has fallen to her knees and offers Jesus her cheek for a kiss, while Joseph examines the wound with concern. Joseph is an older, strong, lean, bearded man, his sleeves rolled up for physical labour. A dark-haired assistant looks at Jesus with the same rapt attention as the others. As Joseph has only one assistant, it's clear he's not running a major business and, as the males are barefoot, there's not much cash to spare. On the wall behind Joseph are arrayed the carpenter's tools including a saw, a set square and an auger drill. Next to them, on a ladder, sits a dove, symbolising the Holy Spirit, the third member of the Holy Trinity: God the Father, God the Son and God the Holy Ghost. Outside, a flock of sheep press against fence-rails as if yearning to get inside: the sheep symbolise the believer for whom Christ is the divine shepherd.

Tekton is an Ancient Greek noun translated in English language Bibles as carpenter. Master carpenters were close to the rather more grand profession of architecture, but Joseph, a figure of humility, was not of that ilk. It was his very ordinariness that makes the story of Christ's early years special. Fellow prophet Buddha was a wealthy, educated man.

Depending on what the job required, carpenters used a variety of trees, including Cypress, Oak, Ash, Sycamore and Olive (*Olea europaea*). If it were a special project, they might have to import expensive Cedar from Lebanon (*Cedrus libani*) or use vines for small projects. When a carpenter needed wood he sliced, with the aid of an assistant, trees into boards using a large bronze saw. Backbreaking labour. Then the trunks were slivered. In Millais's painting, the boards can be seen leaning against the wall behind Joseph. Wood sourcing and cutting were tricky tasks because in that dry region, which lacked forests, trees were often not large or straight. It's work that would make a man strong, fit and practical, and give him a keen eye for detail and balance. 'True' is a word with many meanings but applied to carpentry, it means exact or accurate. Other of its meanings—loyal, faithful, honourable—apply to Joseph himself.

Joseph and his assistant are making a door. Positioned flat on the table, with a bench vice to keep it steady, the door may represent the table of the last supper that Christ had with his disciples, or perhaps an altar. In the Catholic Church, the mass is a miraculous re-enactment of Christ's death, where the bread wafer and the wine that the priest holds aloft are transformed into the body and blood of Christ, the sacrament of communion given by the priest to the church-goer. The prefiguring of blood and suffering, which had its realisation in the Passion of the Christ, saturates Millais's work. The child's fragility and innocence make the horrors ahead even more unsettling. The wood displayed in a variety of objects in the painting can be read, in toto, as a mournful homage to Christianity's most significant symbol—the cross.

Palm Sunday was Jesus's last joyful public event. It was more than joyful, it was triumphant, and it sealed his fate with the resentful, power-hungry Pharisees. As his ascendancy with the populace and his criticism of the priests escalated, the latter were plotting against him. Christ entered Jerusalem on a donkey and the crowds waved, or in some versions placed on the ground, Date Palm fronds. It was a sign of respect, recognising Jesus as a saviour, even a ruler.

It was Passover and Jerusalem was crowded with thousands of pilgrims. Passover celebrated the exodus of Jewish people from Egypt, an event triggered by the seven plagues. Moses had asked for his people to be released from slavery, a request the pharaoh ignored. A wrathful Jehovah then sent the plagues. With the final plague, where all one-year-old children died, Jewish homes were spared, or passed over. Ramses II was probably the pharaoh at the time and according to the Old Testament, he was glad for the Jews to leave. It was the beginning of forty years of wandering, but at least they were free.

Each Passover, pilgrims commemorated the sacred event by visiting the temple, praying and making offerings. The last thing the Roman government or the Pharisees wanted was a riot.

Jesus was a troublemaker. In a spectacular act of righteous anger, he'd chased the moneychangers from the temple.

Gethsemane was the Olive grove where Christ awaited his fate: his betrayal by the apostle Judas and his arrest by an angry, armed mob. It was where he prayed desperately to be delivered from the suffering to come. In this dramatic, tree-oriented event, even Judas has a tree named in his honour: the Judas tree from which, it was believed, he hanged himself after falling into despair due to his treachery.

Gethsemane finds Jesus at his most human. An enclosed, stony Mediterranean garden, it's at the foot of the Mount of Olives. It wasn't the first time Jesus visited: it was already a place of retreat and solace. But that night it was a site of lonely vigil, of fear and spiritual isolation where, 'greatly distressed and troubled', he begged his disciples to 'remain here and watch', telling them, 'My soul is very sorrowful, even unto death.' Famously, they fell asleep.

In Hebrew, *Gethsemane* means oil-press (*gat*, press; *shemen*, oil). Mark 14:32 describes it as a *chorion*, 'a place' or 'field', while John 13:1 speaks of it as *kepos*, 'a garden' or 'orchard'. Ancient Olives continue to grow there in fabulous, twisted shapes. Three of the trees have been radiocarbon dated and it seems that not only do they date from the twelfth century AD, but they are siblings, that is, they come from the one original cutting, a 'mother'.[4] Who knows? Perhaps they are the descendants of the trees of Jesus's time. Given his fate, it's fitting Jesus chose a natural environment in which to spend his last hours of freedom. Trees can offer consolation.

The Olive has its own symbolic tradition. It's regarded as a sign of peaceful entreaty: 'offering the Olive branch'. When Noah sent forth a dove from the Ark to check that the floodwaters had receded, the bird returned with an Olive leaf, a symbol of hope and fecundity.

When I lived in Tuscany, our house, Paretiao, was surrounded by Olive groves. There's scarcely a hillside in Italy that is not replete with them. The trees are on a delightfully human scale and their refined contortions are intriguing to behold. They seem frozen in a moment while dancing and I used to imagine that, one day, if I turned quickly enough, I would catch them at it.

During the harvest season, the branches were weighed down with ripe fruit. Together with Elizabeth Gower and John R Neeson, the artist friends with whom I shared Paretiao, and Judith Blackall, its manager, we carried out the enjoyable task of picking the olives, up ladders in the trees. The olives we took in baskets to the nearby village of Colleoli, where there was an oil press, available to one and all, which turned our olives into a sumptuous, silky liquid that was delicious cooked or raw. The process was as satisfying as catching your own fish and cooking it over a campfire.

Pontius Pilate, the Roman governor, was reluctant to order Christ's torture and death. Nonetheless, to quell the mob (not everyone regarded Jesus as their saviour), Pilate conceded that Jesus must die and 'washed his hands' (literally) of judgement. Christ was then flogged and, in mockery of him being the 'King of the Jews', a crown of thorns was pressed upon his head. Crown of thorns, also called Christ thorn (*Euphorbia splendens* or *Euphorbia milii*), is a thorny, vinelike plant and may be the variety that was used.

Myrrh was also present during Jesus's sufferings. Mark 15:23 writes that Jesus was offered wine and myrrh before the crucifixion: the mixture was meant to have soothing analgesic qualities. But Jesus refused. Perhaps because he wanted no impediment to the pain he was about to experience, the task he was destined to fulfill—the sacrifice of his own life to save humankind. Myrrh is harvested in the same way as frankincense—but from *Commiphora* trees—and originates from the same parts of the world. It derives from the Arabic word for 'bitter'. I've just been burning some myrrh resin, so I agree with that. Despite the interests of research, I will desist from chewing it.

Of the Gospel chroniclers, only John comments that Jesus carried his own cross. Matthew, Mark and Luke refer to Simon of

Cyrene, whom the Roman soldiers grabbed from the crowd and forced to carry, or to assist Jesus in carrying, the cross to Golgotha, which John 19:17 translates as 'the place of skulls'. It must have been a hideous irony for Jesus to drag a wooden cross, an object he would have been familiar with from his own craftsmanship.

The Romans were keen on crucifixion. It was a favoured method of killing criminals, recaptured slaves or whoever they regarded as a threat to the law and order of the Roman Empire. It was unique to the Romans at that point in history. Crucifixion was not only a death sentence, it was designed to humiliate the victims who were often stripped naked and left to rot. The Roman slave Spartacus who led rebellions against the empire, the last in AD 71, was crucified together with thousands of his followers. It could take days to die. Fortunately for Jesus, it was only a matter of hours.

No doubt the crosses were recycled because wood in Israel was scarce. But wood could be sourced from across the entire empire, which stretched through the immense forests of Gaul and Germania, and then hauled to the Middle East.

Jesus is not alone in being a god who died and lived again. The tree gods of Greek mythology, Adonis and Attis, and their relationship to the story of the death and resurrection of Jesus, was first explored by James Frazer in *The Golden Bough*. The twelve-volume opus published between 1890 and 1915 is regarded as a foundation stone of modern anthropology. It's a brilliant piece of research, if you can endure Frazer's arrogant attitudes towards 'heathens' and 'savages'.

Adonis and Attis were handsome youths who met grisly ends. Adonis is an ancient Mediterranean vegetation god: he represented the cycles of nature—birth, death and rebirth—in a sacred form. He was believed to have been torn to pieces by a wild boar, either sent by Artemis (the goddess of the hunt) or Ares (the god of war), take your pick. So 'year by year, when the trees were deciduous' Adonis 'would seem to bleed to death with the red leaves of autumn and to come to life again with the fresh green of spring'.[5]

Easter is the most important festival in the Christian calendar. In the northern hemisphere, it's celebrated around the time of the spring equinox, referencing its qualities of hope, rebirth and revival after the rigours of winter. Frazer also explores the possibility that Adonis was 'sometimes personated by a living man who died a violent death in the character of the god' thus ensuring a successful harvest.[6] Adonis spent several months above the earth (spring and summer) then retreated to the underworld (autumn and winter).

The early Christian Church, in its battle to win the hearts and minds of the pagan population, usurped long-honoured pagan deities, festivals and places or, as Frazer puts it, 'skilfully contrived to plant the seeds of the new faith on the old stock of paganism'. So, the Easter celebration of the dead and risen Christ was 'grafted upon' a similar celebration of the dead and risen Adonis.[7]

Fittingly, one of Europe's oldest trees, so determined in 2016, is named after Adonis. It's a 1079-year-old Bosnian Pine (*Pinus heldreichii*) growing in the Pindos Mountains in northern Greece. Adonis is a gnarled and handsome old fellow flourishing on a bare ridge overlooking a steep hillside. 'Adonis sits in a scraggly region only trafficked by sheepherders and hikers en route to more exciting destinations, but it's still just a few miles from areas that have been inhabited for thousands of years.'[8] Making its longevity even more remarkable.

The tree took root in AD 941. The date is known because Adonis is the type of tree that lays down about one ring each year, so it can be aged quite conclusively. Paul J Krusic, a graduate student from Stockholm University, was a member of the expedition that found the tree. Krusic specialises in a method of tree-ring dating called dendrochronology. He extracted cores from within the tree to count growth rings. The process doesn't harm the plants— the cores themselves are only around 5 millimetres in diameter.

Adonis, 1075-year-old pine, Pindros Mountains, Bosnia, Oliver Kontner, 2016.

'The tree we have stumbled across is a unique individual,' says Krusic. 'It cannot rely on a mother plant, or the ability to split or clone itself, to survive. Cloning is a very effective evolutionary survival strategy. It's not the same as you or I being left alone to our own devices and living for 1000 years, like this tree'.[9]

Attis is also associated with the Pine tree, under which, Frazer tells us, he 'unmanned himself and then bled to death'.[10] Rome worshipped Attis. Emperor Claudius who reigned from AD 41–54 incorporated rituals for the sacred Pine. On 22 March, around the annual spring equinox, a Pine was cut and treated as a divinity. The duty of carrying the tree was entrusted to a guild of tree-bearers. I'll let Frazer describe the scene.

'The trunk was swathed like a corpse with woollen bands and decked with wreaths of violets, for violets were said to have sprung from the blood of Attis … ; and the effigy of a young man, doubtless Attis himself, was tied to the middle of the trunk.' On the Day of Blood (two days later),

> the high priest drew blood from his arms and presented it as an offering. Nor was he alone in this bloody sacrifice. Stirred by the wild barbaric music of clashing cymbals, rumbling drums, droning horns, and screaming flutes, the inferior clergy whirled about in the dance with waggling heads and streaming hair, until, rapt into a frenzy of excitement and insensible to pain, they gashed their bodies with potsherds [sharp ceramic fragments] or slashed them with knives in order to bespatter the altar and the sacred tree with their flowing blood.[11]

Then, following Attis's lead, they castrated themselves.

Thus the Pine tree as a symbol of the living and the dying god is an ancient one. But its appearance as a symbol of the god's birth, at Christmas, rather than his death, is quite recent. A Christmas tree is an evergreen Conifer and it can be Pine, Spruce or Fir, though Pine seems to be the crowd favourite. Indeed, supplying the market with harvested 'Christmas trees' is a healthy business in many parts of the globe.

Ron Junghans has been growing Radiata Pine for the Christmas market since 1979 at his property at Duffys Forest, around 20 kilometres north of Sydney. The Pines are constantly pruned to reach the desired heights of between 1 to 3 metres. That takes about five years. Junghans sells about five hundred trees per season for between $100 and $170 each. It gets quite hectic. Customers are looking for that 'conical shape, nice and green of course, plenty of branches and bushy'.[12]

But the Conifer's history goes back much further than us and our rituals. Hardy Conifers managed to grow in northern Scandinavia during the last Ice Age. The ice was up to 3000 metres thick and covered some 6 million square kilometres of Scandinavia, the United Kingdom, Germany, Poland and western Russia.[13] As Rasmus Kragh Jakobsen writes, 'Up to now, most scientists have subscribed to the general view that the advancing ice presented all living things with an ultimatum: Go south or die out!'[14] Eske Willerslev, from the Centre for Geogenetics at the University of Copenhagen, led a research team which used DNA technology to explore the origins of Scandinavian forests. The theory was that when the last Ice Age started around 115 000 years ago, it was only when the ice melted some 9000 years ago that trees began to re-appear. But sediments found in a lake in central Norway revealed samples of 10 300-year-old DNA, which show the indigenous Scandinavian Spruce (*Picea abies*) was alive and well when the whole country was supposed to be blanketed with ice. The trees had found a refuge which lasted tens of thousands of years.

Celebrating Christmas with a Conifer is a German custom that has become popular since the mid-nineteenth century. The tough evergreen denotes the persistence of life during the demands of

Ron Junghans, Duffy's Forest, NSW, 2016. Reproduced by permission of the Australian Broadcasting Corporation–Library Sales. Amanda Hoh © 2016 ABC.

winter, as well as being a fertility symbol. The Pine can endure the weight of snow due to its needle-like leaves. Pine trees often have both male and female characteristics, making them very efficient in their reproductive, and therefore survival, strategies.[15] The cones make excellent kindling and give off a sharp, refreshing scent.

Having the money to acquire a tree, deck it with ornaments and arrange family presents around its base meant it was a custom only adopted by the affluent classes. But it became the rage in England when Queen Victoria's Christmas tree at Windsor Castle appeared in *The Illustrated London News* in 1848. It's an intimate scene with the Queen and her German husband, Prince Albert, and their family. The little ones are gazing in wonder and delight at the tree, signalling the future market of Christmas's commercial success—children. Equally, the Christmas tree has become a symbol of home, family and sharing.

Queen Victoria's Christmas tree at Windsor Castle, *The Illustrated London News,* 1848, Album/Alamy Stock Photo.

While I think it's a fine thing to celebrate such an important occasion with a tree, it was disturbing to see, after Christmas last year, Elwood littered with dead Pines. The trees don't fit in the rubbish bins and perhaps not many locals have either the will or the implements to chop them up. So about the suburb they lay, like so many carcasses, until the council workers finally collected them. It seemed wasteful, and a little sad, a sign of our throwaway society.

TREE
WORSHIPPERS

AS I WRITE this chapter, it's autumn, or fall, as North Americans name it. Not a bad idea given that's what leaves do from many deciduous trees. If you're wondering about the derivation of 'autumn', it's from the Latin (*autumnus*) and prior to that perhaps Etruscan, suggesting a change or a loss.

Autumn is spectacular in Melbourne. We're famous for it. The leaves of the Liquidambar (*Liquidambar styraciflua*) glow with colours so vivid it seems they are on fire: burnished gold and tangerine, hot bright green, scarlet and bloody burgundy, and all that can happen on one tree. When the sun shines through the leaves, they become luminous. It's as though the leaves catch the light and hold it. What's happening is that the chlorophyll, responsible for producing the tree's energy, is drawn back into the body of the tree. Thus the leaves lose their pale green hue while the red and yellow shades remain. Those colours are always present but they are masked when chlorophyll dominates. It's a sight that is startling, enchanting and melancholic. Autumn might be, in John Keats's words, a season of 'mists and mellow fruitfulness', but it's also a time of withdrawal as the trees indicate what's ahead—brrr! The snap of winter.

Of course, in the southern hemisphere, we experience a winter nothing so brutal as Boston or Reykjavík. As far as winter goes, except for snow falling in the far mountain ranges, we're wimps. 'It's cold!' we moan to one another on frosty mornings. By and large, however, I don't find conversations about the weather banal.

It's an opportunity, as humans, and particularly the city–dwelling variety, to share our feelings about the natural world. We might try to deny it, in our lordly *Homo sapiens,* top–of–the–pecking–order way, but nature always impinges upon us. It draws attention to itself, it frames our days and nights, it quietly and relentlessly continues whether we like it or not. Trees, after all, have been here, evolving, disseminating and travelling, much longer than we have. We should humble ourselves before nature, and learn.

A glorious European Ash (*Fraxinus excelsior*) that grows on the banks of Elster Creek is currently disrobing itself of the massive

European Ash, Elster Creek, Elwood, Janine Burke, 2019.

cloak of shimmering green that it wears during spring and summer, and that spreads down its long arms to the ground. The Ash is so lushly verdant that on a glaring day, its shadowy interior offers an inviting retreat. I'm not the only visitor. Mr and Mrs Blackbird flick the undergrowth for bugs and, during spring, they safely nest amid the tree's camouflage.

Sometimes, Jet, a reserved and sinuous sable puss, who lives nearby with her human companion, can be seen climbing its branches. She sends the birds into a frenzy: they gang up and scream at her until she beats a retreat. On my way to Elwood village for a morning coffee, I often pause beneath the tree. Just stand there silently and feel my feet upon the earth. Still for a while before the day's energy and demands draw me forward.

Have you ever wondered why trees shed? Isn't winter the time to rug up rather than go naked? As Kim Coder points out, 'trees lose their leaves by design'.[1] It's time for them to rest. Growth is stalled and the complex architecture of their bare branches can be viewed. It's a different kind of aesthetic—clean and stark. It reminds how nature schools us in the seasonal varieties of beauty, whether it's rich, dense and blooming or cool, bleak and minimal. In 'Winter Trees', William Carlos Williams describes it thus:

> All the complicated details
> of the attiring and
> the disattiring are completed!
> A liquid moon
> moves gently among
> the long branches.
> Thus having prepared their buds
> against a sure winter
> the wise trees
> stand sleeping in the cold.[2]

The European Ash has an illustrious history. Indeed, in Old Norse and Icelandic cultures, there is no greater tree being. It was worshipped as the World Tree, Yggdrasil. Its roots went down into the earth and its topmost branches up into the sky. Its trunk held the world together like a spine. In its branches it held the nine worlds, including Asgard, the home of the gods where they assembled daily, a kind of Norse Olympus, and Midgard, directly beneath it, the realm of humans—Middle Earth.

There's also a Norse tree creation story. Three gods are strolling along the freshly minted planet Earth when they discover, by the seashore, entwined tree trunks, perhaps pieces of driftwood. While shaped like a man and a woman, they are lifeless. So the gods decide to give them what they lacked and animate them.

> Soul they had not, sense they had not,
> Heat nor motion, nor goodly hue;
> Soul gave Othin, sense gave Hönir,
> Heat gave Lothur and goodly hue[3]

They named the man Ask (Ash) and the woman Embla (Elm). Then Ask and Embla were given Midgard for their dwelling-place and became the parents of the human race. It's a nice story as it encompasses the sea—from where life first came crawling out—and trees. Interestingly, both Ash and Elm—depending on the species—can be bisexual, having male and female seeds and flowers on the same tree. Is this the reference those who told these tales wished to make? That male and female were indeed 'entwined' in the Ash and the Elm?

The Poetic Edda is a collection of Icelandic poems derived from Old Norse mythology which features both the creation tale and Yggdrasil. The history of the poems is mysterious. As translator Nick Richardson comments, 'We don't know when the [*Poetic Edda*] was written … The earliest manuscript dates from the 1270s, but [*The Poetic Edda*] is much older, and the stories are older still. It is generally thought to have been a minstrel poem that was passed down through the centuries by word of mouth'.[4]

The manuscript was kept hidden for centuries. When Christianity became law in Iceland in AD 1000, pagan rituals were punishable by law, making the manuscript a forbidden item. Who knows which pagan families cared for this precious object? They did their job well. The manuscript, with its forty-five calf-skin vellum pages, came to light in 1643 when it was offered to the Lutheran bishop and antiquarian sleuth Brynjólfur Sveinsson. He presented it to King Frederick III of Denmark and it was placed in Copenhagen's Royal Library. But in 1971, after decades of petition-ing by Iceland, it was returned home where it's held in the Árni Magnússon Institute for Icelandic Studies, in Reykjavík. You can see it there.[5] *The Poetic Edda* had finally got its due. Its homecoming was suitably Viking: the manuscript was deemed too precious to return by plane so it was transported by ship, accompanied by a military escort.

In the gorgeously titled 'Völuspá', the first and most significant volume of *The Poetic Edda*, Völvá, a female shaman, tells how the three Fates inhabit the tree and there decide humankind's destiny.

> An Ash I know, Yggdrasil its name,
> With water white is the great tree wet;
> Thence come the dews that fall in the dales,
> Green by Urth's well does it ever grow.
>
> Thence come the maidens mighty in wisdom,
> Three from the dwelling down 'neath the tree;
> Urth is one named, Verthandi the next,—
>
> On the wood they scored,—and Skuld the third.
> Laws they made there, and life allotted
> To the sons of men, and set their fates.[6]

Interestingly, my Ash is a triple tree: three monumental, separate trunks grow from the one base. The Fates perhaps? Urth dealt with the past, Verthandi, the present and Skuld, the future. These giant netherworld goddesses are known as Norn and they live on in literature as the prognosticating witches, 'the weird sisters', of Shakespeare's *Macbeth*.

In *The Poetic Edda*, Völvá prophesises to Odin, a father god similar in status to the Greek Zeus, a series of catastrophic events. A battle—in which fire and flood overwhelm heaven and Earth as the gods fight their enemies—is *ragnarök*, 'the fate of the gods'. But Yggdrasil will survive, and the gods will rise again.

Ragnarök has currency. *Thor: Ragnarok* (2017) is a popular superhero movie based on Marvel Comics's version of the Viking myth. Chris Hemsworth stars as Thor and Cate Blanchett as his sister Hela.[7] It grossed US$854 million worldwide. So indeed the gods have risen again.

If you're a JRR Tolkien fan you'll recall that in *The Hobbit*, the powerful wizard Gandalf carries a wand which also serves as a staff and a weapon. Tolkien was highly influenced by the 'Völuspá', not only because it was a primary source for German legend and Norse myth, but its amalgam of Old Norse and Icelandic provided the basis for his own Middle Earth fantasy language, Mannish.

Völvá was the female archetype of Gandalf—indeed, in the 'Völuspá', she lists the names of the dwarves: Gandalf means 'wand elf', Völvá means 'wand carrier' or, in Icelandic, the more romantic, 'wand-wed'. Tolkien also borrowed these names for his dwarves, offering an historic resonance to a contemporary text.

I wonder whether—given Völvá was identified with Yggdrasil, and her name signifies that her talents as a seer were epitomised by her wand—the staff she carried was made from the Ash, emphasising its sacred role in Icelandic culture?

There's a problem with my theory and it has to do with Iceland's tree history. Iceland is a brutal and beautiful place, a land of fire and ice, of glaciers and volcanoes, of austere rolling hills and icy waterfalls, of the Northern Lights that bejewel the winter sky like diaphanous, green, cosmic curtains. Iceland's wild, visual majesty has become better known since segments of *Game of Thrones*, the enormously popular TV series set in a medieval dystopia, were filmed there. Winter's force, essayed with such gruelling detail in the series, gave a new emphasis to the word cold, while the gloomy prophecy 'Winter is coming!' became a catch phrase. A thriving tourist industry to the little island—the population has only recently nudged over 350 000—has resulted.

The Vikings were intrepid sailors who made the 1400-kilometre crossing over the North Atlantic to the island in the ninth century AD. Unlike Australia, with its centuries of Indigenous occupation, Iceland *was* terra nullius. Its culture grew from the Vikings, as well as the other arrivals, including the Celts, and their Irish slaves known as thralls, with whom the Vikings intermingled. But Iceland did develop its own native language. *The Poetic Edda* came to be written in an era when Iceland strived to establish its cultural autonomy. Over the centuries, it was governed by the superior powers of Norway and Denmark. It achieved independence in 1918.

When the Vikings arrived, from what is now known as Norway, they set about deforesting the country. Probably about 60 per cent of Iceland's forests were lost in the next two hundred years. By the 1950s, 1 per cent was left. Thus Iceland has virtually no old growth forests. There's a joke—'If you get lost in an Iceland forest, stand up'. It's easy to blame the Vikings, but they needed to protect their families, build homes and light fires as well as clear the land for crops such as hay and barley. Deforestation has been a feature of human cultures for millennia, though it's only now, in our time, that it has become a most dangerous practice, a hazard for the future of the planet.

While admitting that Iceland's deforestation is one of the worst in the world, Þröstur Eysteinsson, director of the Icelandic Forest Service, is cautiously optimistic about the future.[8] But which trees to plant? These days the soil is first tested before the most suitable tree for planting is selected, often Sitka Spruce (*Picea sitchensis*) or Lodgepole Pine (*Pinus contorta*). The reason is that in the 1950s, Siberian Larch (*Larix sibirica*) was planted but many died off, while the Birch native to Iceland, *Betula pubescens*, struggled to cope with the climate shifts of global warming. The soil's poor quality, eroded by centuries of sheep munching the vegetation down to bare earth, meant that, once exposed, it was susceptible to frosts and erosion—the wind simply blew it away. Further, eruptions over the ensuing centuries from the many volcanoes deposited thick layers of volcanic material, creating deserts. As a result, Iceland is a case study in desertification, with little or no vegetation, though the problem is not heat or drought.

The Icelandic Forest Service runs a large seed nursery available to those wishing to replant for the timber industry, home building or just to nourish the land. However, the re-greening is a long, slow process and it will probably take about 150 years to truly make a difference.

How does the Ash fit into this picture? Despite its centrality to Icelandic myth, the Ash is unknown as a native tree there. Ditto, the Elm. Birch, yes. Rowan, some. But these are not gigantic trees. They are *not* Yggdrasil. The farthest north the Ash has been found is in Norway at a latitude that connects with southern Iceland. Did the Vikings try to plant the Ash and found that Iceland's soil was inhospitable? Is Yggdrasil a symbol or a memory of the forests that once graced the island? Or is it a sentimental longing by the new settlers for the lands they had left behind, with their grand forests and sacred groves, trees big enough to inspire mystical connections? We can only guess.[9]

There is, however, proof that the wand-wed witches of Scandinavia existed. Archaeological finds indicate the esteem in which women prophets were held. In one find, known as the Fyrkat Seeress, and held in the Danish National Museum, is the grave of a woman.[10] It's perhaps from around AD 970. The Fyrkat Seeress was dressed in finely woven blue and red clothes adorned with gold thread, giving her royal status. She was buried in a wooden carriage, like upper-class women. She also wore silver toe-rings, an unusual and costly item of decoration. Her wand was placed in her grave, lying next to her. Partially disintegrated after its long burial, it's a dainty iron stick with bronze fittings. Wood deteriorates over time so the canny witch had hers made of something more durable.

I wonder if the Fyrkat Seeress foresaw the fate of her fellows? Not only were pagan practices banned under Christian law, but in the seventeenth century the sorcery trials began. Known in Iceland as the Age of Fire and taking place between 1654 and 1690, over two hundred people were charged with either practising magic or being in possession of magical items. Of them, twenty-one were burned at the stake: twenty men and one woman. It takes a lot of wood to build and maintain a pyre—a gruesome statistic, I know. How hideously ironic for the witches that they were killed by something pagans worshipped—the tree.

But, rather like the gods of *ragnarök*, paganism has re-emerged. As I write this in September 2020, a temple honouring the old gods is being built on the outskirts of Reykjavík. Plans show a dramatically modern building set into a rocky slope and surrounded by a forest of young Pines. It will hold a capacity of two hundred. The architect Magnús Jensson and project adviser Hilmar Örn Hilmarsson are both members of Iceland's pagan movement, known as Ásatrú (faith in the gods). They regard the site as sacred.

Ásatrú championed the Icelandic Forest Service's scheme to reforest parts of the country, where three million trees are being planted annually mainly for the good of nature but also, potentially, for timber production. Some of the older trees in the scheme will be used to make the temple's roof. 'It will be the first building made from Icelandic timber,' Hilmarsson claims proudly. 'It's only in the last few years that we've had trees big enough to produce timber in Iceland.'[11]

Each piece of wood, and each hewn rock, are deemed holy. 'We have a long history for not wanting to disturb certain rocks because we knew there were elves in them,' says Hilmarsson, 'and even people who don't believe in them pay lip service because it's better to be on the safe side'.[12]

Already in love with words as an eleven-year-old, I then fell in love with a dictionary. Not just any dictionary. A great, thick chunk of a dictionary. A Webster's. In those days, the early 1960s, people sold items door to door (encyclopaedias and vacuum cleaners most notably). I think that's how my family came to own it because in 1961, Webster's (today known as Merriam-Webster) was re-issued as the *Third New International Dictionary*. It was too big to hold on my knees, it must have weighed several kilos, so I lay on my stomach on the living-room floor and trawled its pages, its deep, delicious draughts of wordy knowledge.

On the inside cover, I found a tree, a picture of all the languages in the world. Yggdrasil no less. Its roots were inscribed with the word Proto-Indo-European while its trunk and branches were decorated with the names Germanic, Anglo-Frisian, Ugric, right to the top tips of English, Hindi and Italian. An intensely visual creature, even as a child, it was a treat not only to read but to see the tree of language. Words are things, too. They can be heard and admired, and, as John Keats wrote, 'A thing of beauty is a joy forever'.

So, what does 'tree' mean? Of course, it's an ancient word and it's undergone various changes as the centuries go by and as languages travel and permutate. It's true source is not only debatable but literally unknown. Here are some of the best guesses.

There's Old English *treo*, *treow* meaning tree, wood, timber, beam, log, stake, stick, grove and cross. *Treow* derives from Proto-Germanic *trewq* (source of Old Frisian *tre*, Old Saxon *trio*, Old Norse *tre*, Gothic *triu*) and, a hugely long way back, from Proto-Indo-European *doru*, the suffixed variant form of the root *deru*—be firm, solid, steadfast.

Proto-Indo-European, or PIE, was spoken by a people who lived from roughly 4500 to 2500 BC, a Bronze Age culture that left no written texts. The website given in this endnote will provide you with an opportunity to hear how it may have sounded, rather lovely and sibilant.[13]

Perhaps the tree of language was one of the incentives that encouraged me to decide, at that age, to become a writer.

While the Ash has a venerable and sacred history, it has an uncertain future. Once a popular garden and street tree, it was

The Tree of Languages, Guy Holt, 2020.

widely cultivated in the temperate regions of New Zealand. But its propensity to crowd out native trees and dominate the waterways mean it's now regarded as a pest in some parts. Indeed, a weed. A weed, I might add, is merely a plant growing where humans object to it growing.

NAMING TREES

THERE'S A HIGH storm thrashing Elwood and I'm in the kitchen watching the Silver Birch hit the windows; its leafless branches (it's winter) are like strands of long, wild, tawny hair. *Don't break the windows*, I beg the tree silently. *Firstly, it would make a dreadful mess and secondly, we might have to trim you,* Betula pendula, *and you'd look peculiar shorn.*

The tree's reckless power and its ability to arouse fear and wonder make me consider the ways in which we symbolise nature's intentions in order to understand them, to include ourselves in them and attempt to placate them.

The Tree (2010) is a feature film based on Judy Pascoe's novel *Our Father Who Art in the Tree* (2002), and subtly directed by Julie Bertuccelli. Dawn, played by Charlotte Gainsbourg, is suddenly widowed when her husband (Aden Young) has a heart attack and crashes his ute into the enormous Moreton Bay Fig (*Ficus macrophylla*) next to their Queensland home. Their eight-year-old daughter Simone (Morgana Davis), refusing to grieve, is convinced that the spirit of her father now inhabits the tree. Dawn, engulfed by sadness and facing the prospect of raising four children alone, is intrigued by her daughter's unshakeable faith.

When Dawn starts dating George (Marton Csokas), her new boss, Simone is angry and jealous. Does the tree share her feelings?

One night, a huge branch crashes through a window and on to Dawn's bed. She's out of the room at the time. Dawn doesn't remove the branch but curls up next to it. When George comes to inspect the damage, he's bemused. 'Have you been sleeping with it, then?' he asks. To his comment, 'Lucky it didn't hurt you', Dawn replies in astonishment, 'Oh, I don't think it meant to harm me!' The tree has become the body of her husband, the intimate sharer of her bed, a symbol of the strength of memory and love, and of nature's power to console.

Standing beneath a Moreton Bay Fig on Elster Creek is to recognise the differing and conflicting powers that Bertuccelli's film seeks to convey—awe at the tree's majesty, which suggests scant concern for puny humans and our concerns, and its invitingly broad, low branches which, for the adventurous or the child, would be easy to climb. The tree offers a paradoxical combination of might with an architecture that is accommodating, even welcoming. Such paradoxical qualities are evident in a medicine that Aboriginal people prepare from its milky sap, one of its many uses they have found. The sap is mixed with other ingredients to make a tincture to treat infections and to dress small wounds, but if the sap comes into contact with the skin unadulterated, it's an irritant.

The tree's glossy leaves are the size of your hand. Beneath live parasites, colonies of thrip which cluster in rows and make a tiny canopy, or gall, under which they eat and sleep, and which blackens and destroys the leaf that is their host. However, the Fig is so vigorous that it takes its unpleasant guests in its stride, as if such miniscule creatures aren't worth bothering about. The Fig is a fighter. Currently it's strangling a Canary Island Date Palm (*Phoenix canariensis*) that sits next to it, denying it light and growth, while the Palm lays its branches across the Fig's as if in supplication.

Beneath the Fig is a thick lawn of ivy and a bevy of ferns. The tree has engineered another ecosystem, as grass cannot thrive in its shade. A Eucalypt, which is next to the Palm, is a match

Moreton Bay Fig, Elwood, Janine Burke, 2018.

for the Fig, racing it towards the sky. But some of the Eucalypt's topmost branches are dead. Perhaps the Fig will eventually win that round, too.

If I were in a Queensland rainforest, among the birds I'd glimpse enjoying the tree's fruit might include the Rose-Crowned Fruit Dove, the Green Catbird, the Satin Bowerbird or the Figbird. While I may not spot the Fruit Dove, a pretty creature who is inconspicuous and well camouflaged, I'd certainly notice the Green Catbird, a species of bowerbird, who meows like a kitten in distress. The wailing is not merely operatic: it's part of a mating ritual where the male announces his territory and warns off intruders.

But, as I'm in Elwood, my companions are two Common Mynas who laugh at me from the branches, a gurgling satiric chuckle that, if you observe them closely, these unloved birds will often direct at you. It's as though they know we resent them as interlopers, an introduced species from southern India, who are reviled for their aggression and their ability to chase native birds from their habitat. There are some local folk who set traps for them, then drown the captives. My attitude is not so severe. The Mynas did not ask to be brought here. They came, they pillaged and they thrived. As did many colonists.

The Fig takes its name from Moreton Bay, an area that includes the mouth of the Brisbane River, where the city of Brisbane now stands, up to Bribie Island in the north and South Stradbroke Island in the south. The Fig is native to that part of the Queensland coast and into northern New South Wales. Lieutenant James Cook named the stretch of water after Lord Morton when Cook sailed along the coastline in the *Endeavour* in May 1770. But the name was wrongly spelled in its first publication and it has remained Moreton Bay ever since.[1]

Lord Morton was president of the Royal Society or, as it was originally known, The Royal Society of London for Improving Natural Knowledge, an august scientific organisation that has existed since the seventeenth century. Cook had reason to feel grateful to Morton. Under his auspices, the Royal Society had engaged Cook to travel to the Pacific Ocean ostensibly to observe the transit of Venus in Tahiti. In fact, Cook's mission was to search for Terra Australis Incognita (unknown southern land).

A month before sailing that stretch of coast, in April 1770, Cook made landfall at Botany Bay, announcing the beginning of white settlement. Cook's process of charting—and naming—the coastline, together with the English explorers who followed him, led, by and large, to the nullification of Indigenous mappings.

Moreton Bay's Aboriginal name is Quandamooka, a region which takes in Mulgumpin (Moreton Island) and its traditional owners, the Ngugi people of the Gowar language.[2] The Ngugi used the Fig's inner bark to weave mesh carry bags as well as scoop fishing nets to catch Red Mullet, turtle and Dugong—a shy, large, underwater mammal. Perhaps the Ngugi also ate the Fig's fruit which is not only plentiful but edible. However, if you expect to taste the sweet flesh of the Common Fig (*Ficus carica*), you'll be disappointed.

Who named it the Moreton Bay Fig? It wasn't Matthew Flinders who landed in the area in July 1799 on the sloop *Norfolk*, sailing up from Sydney. Flinders was travelling with Bungaree, an Aboriginal man from Broken Bay, an 'undaunted fellow' who acted as guide, translator and negotiator for Flinders.[3] So, fortunately for Flinders, he was able to communicate with the Indigenous people he met on Mulgumpin and in the Quandamooka region. Bungaree went on to circumnavigate Australia with Flinders in 1801–02 and had a town on Bribie Island named after him, a rare honour for an Indigenous guide.

In Quandamooka, Flinders and his crew cut down Cedar 'of a fine Grain' (probably Red Cedar, *Toona ciliata* var. *australis*) for firewood. He also saw 'very pretty' wooded islands as well as thickly growing grey mangroves, which so thoroughly blocked the mouth of the Brisbane River that it eluded him. He also noted other 'large and luxuriant trees'.[4]

Were they Moreton Bay Figs? How do trees get named?

The Moreton Bay Fig's official taxonomic name is *Ficus macrophylla* meaning large-leafed Fig (Latin: *ficus*, a Fig tree; Greek: *macro*, large; *phyllus*, leaf). Once its taxonomic name has been published, the tree enters the world stage, so to speak. Since 1867, plant names have been regulated by an International Code of Botanical Nomenclature. But it wasn't a free-for-all before then. Carl Linnaeus systematised two-module name tags and imposed them on nearly six thousand plants in his influential two-volume *Species Plantarum* published in 1753.

Ficus macrophylla was coined by René Desfontaines in 1804 but first described by Christiaan Hendrik Persoon in 1806, so when you find *Desf. x Pers.* after *Ficus macrophylla* that's what it means. Desfontaines came up with the name but it was a *nomen nudum*—a name without a description.[5] That legacy belongs to Persoon who described it, correctly, as a native of New Holland (as Australia was then known).[6]

Though both men were based in Paris, their lives could not have been more dissimilar: Desfontaines was the director of Jardin des Plantes, and was a respected public figure who received prestigious appointments and a variety of awards, while Persoon dwelt in obscurity, a recluse of small means, leading 'a poverty-stricken life devoted to fungi'.[7] Persoon doubtless visited the Jardin des Plantes, the botanical gardens in the heart of Paris. He certainly read Desfontaines's catalogue of the museum's vast herbarium where he named *Ficus macrophylla*.[8] How either Desfontaines or Persoon acquired a specimen of the Moreton Bay Fig remains a mystery— from some botanically minded French traveller to Australian shores, perhaps.

In Australia, the name Moreton Bay Fig was common parlance by 1875 when Walter Hill, director of Brisbane Botanic Gardens, published it in his plant catalogue, though Edward Vidler notes 'the natives called it Waabie'—Waabie is a Gowar word.[9]

Did you know that trees can be valued in monetary terms?

A Moreton Bay Fig in Melbourne's Fawkner Park has been valued at $1.7 million. It's been growing there since 1888. The tree's valuation is worked out using a formula based on its size, health, vigour, canopy balance and contribution to the landscape. In fact, the city's 77000 trees have been valued at $770 million. It's reassuring to know that 677 trees across the municipality are currently covered by tree protection bonds, which means that if a property developer comes along and wants to clear them, they're safe.

Recently, Nina Rønsted and her colleagues have estimated that the Moreton Bay Fig originated at least 41 million years ago and radiated gradually about 35 million years ago.[10] Gondwana was breaking up then. Australia was severing itself from Antarctica and beginning its drift north towards the equator. During that leisurely journey, paced at a few centimetres a year, it experienced major climatic shifts that resulted in cycles of expanding and contracting rainforests.

During the early Miocene (23 to 16 million years ago) northern Australia had a warm, wet climate and was covered in rainforest. *Ficus macrophylla* was there. So was the Fig wasp. Figs are only pollinated by female Fig wasps and only Fig wasps can reproduce in its fruit. So tree and insect have a crucial, dependent relationship known as mutualism, or as Jeff Ollerton has dubbed it, 'biological barter'.[11]

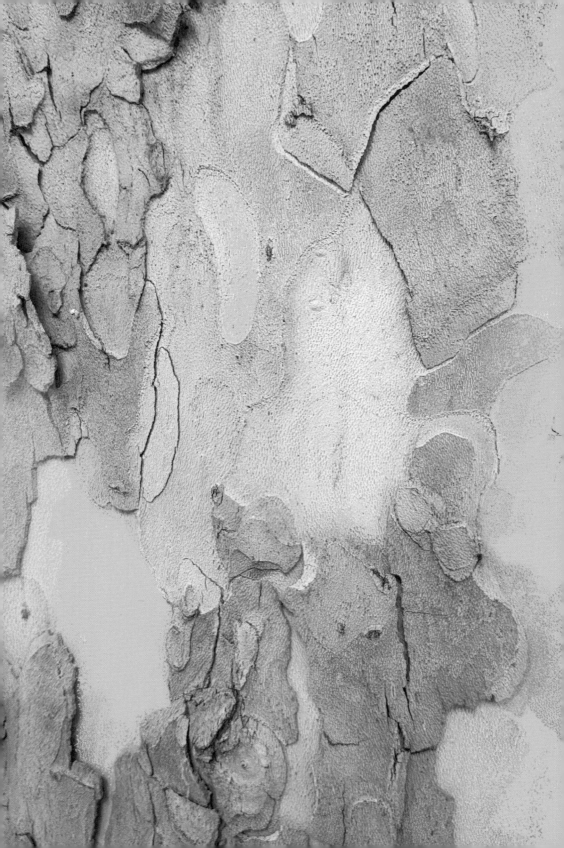

KNOWING TREES

WHEN I LIVED in Tuscany, my writing companion was a Fig. I had left almost everything behind in Melbourne: my family and friends, my job as an art history lecturer at the Victorian College of the Arts and the house I rented in Carlton. All my furniture and other worldly goods were stored in a hangar-sized shed near Melbourne Airport. And then there was Anthony, with the calm visage of an angel, and a personality to match, whose heart I broke. I could not be the woman he wanted me to be, the one who would marry him and have his children. I tore my life apart because I could no longer acquit that safe and orderly existence, with its couples and comforts and certainties. Writing a novel was the rope I grasped and that would take me god knew where but far from where I was.

Before you congratulate me or enviously contemplate a writer's life in Tuscany, let me tell you it was a difficult and painful period where I felt, most of the time, alone and depressed. Part of that sadness was triggered by the death of my grandmother, who had held my world together. I only discovered that when she died. I often felt myself to be beneath the earth, buried in darkness and fear, yearning for oblivion. Freud called mourning 'work', one of the most perceptive comments I've come across.[1] It is work. Hard work.

So that's how I came to be living at Paretiao, a restored farm-house, which was owned by the artist Arthur Boyd and his wife Yvonne. The Boyd family generously loaned the house to creative folk, selected by the Australia Council for the Arts, for several months each year. I'd been awarded a residency and it was how I managed to run away from my former life. It was quite a shock to have had an existence cushioned by predictability, and a good salary, to find myself living in a house in the middle of rural Italy without an income, writing a novel. I could scarcely speak the language. I began *Second Sight* there, and the landscape seeped into the book as dawn's light does into your bedroom, slowly but irrevocably.[2]

Let me describe it for you. It's evening and Lucida, the protagonist, has just made her arrival.

> I watched the sunset colour the sky from the livingroom windows. A fig tree swirled, budding and leafing. Beyond it was a vegetable garden with tomatoes climbing on sticks and silverbeet in profusion like tropical plants. Lettuces, close-packed as petals, dotted the garden's aisles and parsley, wide-leafed as clover, fanned the perimeter. The garden sat on a terrace, the last foothold before the land fell away to the valley. I had a sensation of being up very high, and safe. The stillness had a living quality. Birds made ready for the night, their calls counterpointing with a landscape as it settled to blissful rest. It was as though at that precise moment a curtain had been drawn back to reveal the perfect ending: radiant, ineffable light. I wept in slow breaths. When I stopped night had come, closing one circle, opening another. The house was full of deep shadows slumbering easily. Light clung to edges.[3]

Outside my upstairs window was the massive Fig tree with whom I fell in love. It was not a Moreton Bay, of course. It was deciduous. Probably *Ficus carica*, which originated in Asia and has been cultivated in Europe since the fifteenth century. The elegant tracery of its branches, seen to best advantage in winter, plus the glistening green of its leaves in the other seasons, together with its scale, both in width and height, was mesmerising. Often I would pause as I wrote and just gaze at the tree. Its beauty made friendship possible.

Does that sound odd? As an art historian, my eye is trained in the complex pleasures of the gaze. What is opulent, or ugly, or stupendous, or provocative, or disquieting, makes an intense impression on me, as I study and absorb its aesthetic, and try to put it into words.

Virginia Woolf may not have helped me become an art historian but she helped me as a writer. Her control of language and emotion is so profound it calls attention to the business of writing itself and to the mercurial, incandescent process of creativity. I think Virginia's prose can bewitch one into making art which is, fundamentally, about magic and spirit. Picasso knew that.

The Olive Grove, Paretiao, Tuscany, John R Neeson, 1983.

In 1971, I was an undergraduate majoring in what was known as 'English', as if that one, world-dominating language could represent all global literatures. It was when I read *To the Lighthouse* (1927). I'm glad I found Virginia because the rest of the course seemed stuffy and laborious. Subjecting something as lovely as her prose to academic autopsy, the forensic analysis of the heartbeat of her art, did not agree with me. So, I dropped English and swam into the wide sea of art history. That course was pretty stuffy, too, but at least I had genius to gaze upon—the Renaissance, for example—and the dislocations and demanding energies of modern art.

I still have the same dog-eared copy of *To the Lighthouse*, which has made it off the bookshelf for the first time in many a long year. It's here beside me on my desk. In the frontispiece, I've written my name and beneath it—furiously crossed out—is 'English'. I clearly desired to liberate Woolf from the shackles of the course and position her within my own realm, my personal pantheon of admired authors. These days, there's a fashion for pitching out everything in your home that seems worn, old, irrelevant. Don't do it, is my advice. How could I have known that, nearly fifty years later, I would need this very copy to flesh out my book?

I see I've underlined the final paragraph. It concerns artist Lily Briscoe.

> She looked at her canvas; it was blurred. With a sudden intensity, as if she saw it clear for a second, she drew a line there, in the centre. It was done; it was finished. Yes, she thought, laying down her brush with extreme fatigue, I have had my vision.[4]

The book's cover shows a Matisse-like interior by Ceri Richards. A woman wearing a voluminous red skirt leans against a decoratively painted mantelpiece. Though the woman's features are sketchy, she nonetheless seems thoughtful, reflective. Following Matisse's lead, the composition is a series of attractive, abstracted ovoid shapes.[5]

I vainly hoped Ceri was a woman artist. But no, he's Welsh and, though a contemporary of the Bloomsbury set, not one of their number. Other of Woolf's novels published in the Penguin Modern Classics series—*Mrs Dalloway* (1925) and *The Waves* (1931)—have, on their covers, portraits of Virginia by Vanessa Bell, her elder sister. It was how I came to learn of Vanessa's oeuvre, too. I was on the hunt for women artists, even then. Interesting that my first job after completing my degree was to curate *Australian Women Artists: 1840–1940*, one of the first surveys of the women artists of my country.

Virginia helped me to find my vision. I was impressed by the plangent rhythms of her prose, not only fiction but her essays, diaries and letters and by the quiet but deeply felt exultation that flows through her work which suggests but does not depend on mysticism. Then there's her subject matter, which concerns the unpredictable flows of the inner life, 'myriad impressions—trivial, fantastic, evanescent ... From all sides they come, an incessant shower of innumerable atoms'.[6] Complementing the subject matter is the structural originality of the novels, almost shapeless in form, like water flowing, yet utterly grounded, connected to the Earth itself. You feel you've discovered something fresh and quite startling that speaks directly to your unconscious mind, that rich realm which we, as writers, treasure.

Given my own experience with depression, I also admired Virginia's purpose, to cast off its shroud after her periodic breakdowns, and return to the world, bringing with her art that is not only clever and witty but adamant in its ambition. Perhaps because of that, I continue to find my way back to Virginia. And here she is again, popping up in this book. What can she teach me about nature?

Woolf experienced a rapturous, sensual delight in the natural world. Her home with her husband Leonard in Sussex was a retreat which she loved but which she struggled to fully communicate. In her essay 'Evening over Sussex: Reflections in a motor car', she writes that the beauty of nature is so overwhelming that it cannot be adequately contained by prose. 'I cannot hold this—I cannot express this—I am overcome by it—I am mastered.'[7] There was the 'pure delight' which was before her eyes 'at this very moment' in Sussex. 'The lemon-coloured leaves on the elm tree; the apples in the orchard; the murmur and rustle of the leaves … While I write this, the light glows; an apple becomes a vivid green; I respond all through me; but how?'[8]

Virginia and Leonard bought Monk's House, in the village of Rodmell, in 1919. Virginia was thrilled. 'This will be our address for ever and ever.'[9] When they moved in, Virginia yielded to a 'profound pleasure at the size & shape & fertility & wildness of the garden' with its 'infinity of fruitbearing trees'. It also had well-kept rows of peas, artichokes, potatoes and raspberry bushes with 'pale little pyramids of fruit'. Virginia knew Leonard would become 'a fanatical lover of that garden'.[10]

They holidayed at Rodmell until their apartment in Mecklenburgh Square was bombed in 1940. Then they moved there permanently.

Now owned by the National Trust and open to the public, Monk's House is near the end of the village next to the twelfth-century St Peter's Church and its graveyard: the area has changed little over the decades. Virginia told a friend, 'It seems to me that all the virtues and all the humanities can only flourish in a country village. Don't you think human beings improve very much spaced out with fields between them? And then nature—no, I shall never say how much I adore and respect nature.'[11]

For Virginia, home and garden represented only part of her pleasure in country life. After she finished writing for the day, she went walking or cycling across the Downs, no matter what the weather. Such outings were a necessary part of her creative rhythm. Confined to bed with one of her migraines, she mused,

what wouldn't I give to be coming through Firle woods, dusty & hot, with my nose turned home, every muscle tired, & the brain laid up in sweet lavender, so sane & cool, & ripe for

the morrows task. How I should notice everything—the phrase
for it coming the moment after & fitting like a glove; & then
on the dusty road, as I ground my pedals, so my story would
begin telling itself.[12]

I've made the journey to Monk's House, so I have an inkling of
what Virginia meant. On my quest, I stayed at Lewes, the nearest market town, a handsome and prosperous place with a river
running through, where Virginia and Leonard did their shopping.
More importantly, Lewes had a train station that served East Sussex
and London. From Lewes, I caught a bus that went to Rodmell
on an infrequent timetable, and finally tramped through the
pretty little village on shanks's pony. Rodmell was certainly not
a tourist mecca.

The National Trust has an unusual but pragmatic policy: it publicly advertises many of its homes for tenancy for a ten-year period.
The tenancy for Monk's House had been advertised in the *Evening
Standard*. 'How would you like to look after a garden and share
your house with 7,000 visitors a year?' it read.[13] Caroline Zoob
rang Jonathan, her husband, the minute she spotted it. The couple
were not professional gardeners, but they were keen amateurs and
wanted something more challenging than their postage stamp–
sized London garden.

That's how I met Jonathan, because the tenants have to commit
to being present at the open days. A bevy of volunteers bustled
about, guiding visitors to this or that aspect of the property. The
whole enterprise had a delightfully amateurish air. No smooth
corporate-style organisation here.

Jonathan was taking tickets at a desk near the front door, and
was very cheerful. He and Caroline lived upstairs, sequestered from
the 'vintage' (read public) section of the house, with the necessary
mod cons, but, I would say, without very much space. If you had
children—yikes!—there would be no room for them. Given the
dramas that went on at the house—Virginia's breakdowns and,
in 1941, her suicide—I expected it to have a rather gloomy air,

a resonance of sad times. But it felt joyful, a living memory of Virginia and Leonard's devotion to one another.

Jonathan told me, 'So many visitors comment on the resident cats, the odd sound or the smell of baking from … the kitchen … [and the] signs that the garden is tended by people who really love it—the signs of life in the house'.[14]

The Zoobs's responsibilities included the maintenance and planting of the garden. Jonathan noted, 'On a lovely autumn morning I might stroll out into the Orchard (much as Leonard and Virginia must have done) and pick a few shiny apples to place in the wooden bowl in the dining table, and so the exhibition is constantly enriched in a way that might not happen in an unoccupied museum'. As Monk's House is open twice a week for seven months of the year, the Zoobs employed a conservation cleaner to prepare it for the open days. But having the opportunity 'to enjoy two acres of the most beautiful land in the country is worth the eternal dusting and administrative headaches of finding four volunteers for every opening!'[15]

Virginia wrote in a little weatherboard study. Known as her garden work-lodge, it's at the end of the garden, under the chestnut tree and next to the churchyard wall. Virginia exulted in the view of the lush water-meadows and the Downs. So neat, it seems a modest space to contain such a gigantic mind. It was Virginia's room of her own. While it's scrupulously tidy these days, when Virginia occupied it, it was a creative mess of papers, pens, books and cigarette butts. She wrote on a board on her lap, longhand, rather than on a desk. But during winter, the lodge was freezing and Virginia retreated to her bedroom to write.

In 1923, Woolf's short story 'In the Orchard' was published.[16] Miranda, summer-somnolent, drifts to sleep beneath the Apple trees. Voices are carried like seeds upon the air from the nearby church and school along with the sad lone cry of a drunken man, and germinate in Miranda's mind. In this enchanting reverie, where nature casts an irrevocable spell, Miranda/Virginia can only listen and experience in her blissful daze, all that is around

Virginia Woolf's garden work-lodge, Monk's House, Rodmell, Sussex, Janine Burke, 2008.

her, nature's exquisite—and sometimes dissonant—harmonies. Random thoughts drift through her mind as she senses the busyness of nature. 'A wagtail flew diagonally from one corner to another. Cautiously hopping, a thrush advanced towards a fallen apple; from the other wall a sparrow fluttered just above the grass.'[17]

What was Virginia's reserve about trying to express/clarify/ analyse the ineluctable presence, presents and pressures of nature? It's not enough to describe nature. That can reduce what is marvellous to a metaphor, a synonym, while nature is expansive, mysterious, immanent and inexplicable, capable of answering every definition and yet defying them all. Did it push Woolf towards suggesting that nature was a place of spiritual renewal? Isn't that what beauty can do? Inspire worship? Of course, for a modernist like Woolf whose literary project was as much about formal structural change in the novel as a new kind of subject matter, typifying herself in 'religious' terms would have been anathema. Her writing lodge may have been smack bang next to the church but Virginia did not attend services. In fact, the church bells irritated her—'intermittent, sullen, didactic'—and she disliked them both for what they represented and for their noise.[18]

The rabid nationalism which helped to provoke World War I and the barbarity that followed (one of the first, and worst, episodes of conflict that humanity had collectively experienced) made many artists turn away from viewing art through the prism of religion. Where was God? Surely dead. Religion, and matters of the spirit, were, by and large, not part of the avant-garde. Many modernist intellectuals prided themselves on, if not cool rationality, then at least disdain for the conservative hierarchies and dogmas of the Christian church, as well as its notions of moral conduct. But could nature function as a sort of answer, a reprieve, from either believing in transcendence, or not?

There was only one religion that Freud did not castigate and dismiss, and that was animism, the faith of Indigenous people. The Catholic Church, whose presence dominated Vienna in his day, particularly earned his scorn. Well and good. But what if, on a flight of fantasy, drifting through nature, rather like Miranda on that summer's day, you come across something liminal, elusive, yet potent and memorable? It's not human. It's nature. But more than that. Deeper than that. It's a presence that seems intimate yet other, within and everywhere, immediate and endless. You feel it. It sees you. Then the experience blurs, shivers and disappears, and you're left wondering what has occurred. So, you return to nature, time and again, aware, curious, tantalised. Following the path that sometimes leads to a dead end. It's one of the reasons I'm writing this book—isn't it the reason we write our books?—to try to understand, to put into words and thus share experiences which seem almost impossible to grasp or explain.

My Tuscan Fig inspired me to tell the story of my novel, at least part of it, through the medium of the natural world. *Second Sight* is an autobiographical work: it included my feelings of loss after my grandmother's death, my leave-taking of Melbourne and my arrival in dolce Toscana. I also allowed the symbolism of myth to tell the tale, employing a kind of magical realism, where Judith Blackall, Paretiao's capable and good-hearted manager, became the goddess Artemis, while a sculptor friend Domenico de Clario, also resident at Paretiao, personified as Apollo, Artemis's brother. It was a difficult process as I wrangled the complex messages that nature sent me, the incredible beauty, the massive amount of information, the care and protection that nature sometimes offers together with the barrage of problems and reversals it can let (literally) rain down upon one's head.

Did I compete with the Fig tree for a similar aesthetic effect? Not really because I would only fail. The tree diminished and expanded me, both at once. It offered me precise and exquisite beauty with the rider that I could never match its effect. Never 'master' it. *Second Sight* was a troublesome novel and I went on writing it in Paris and Sydney and rural Victoria, but I held on to the rope, and the book won a literary prize, and suddenly I was solvent again. And I have never forgotten what the Fig tree offered me, and what I learned from it.

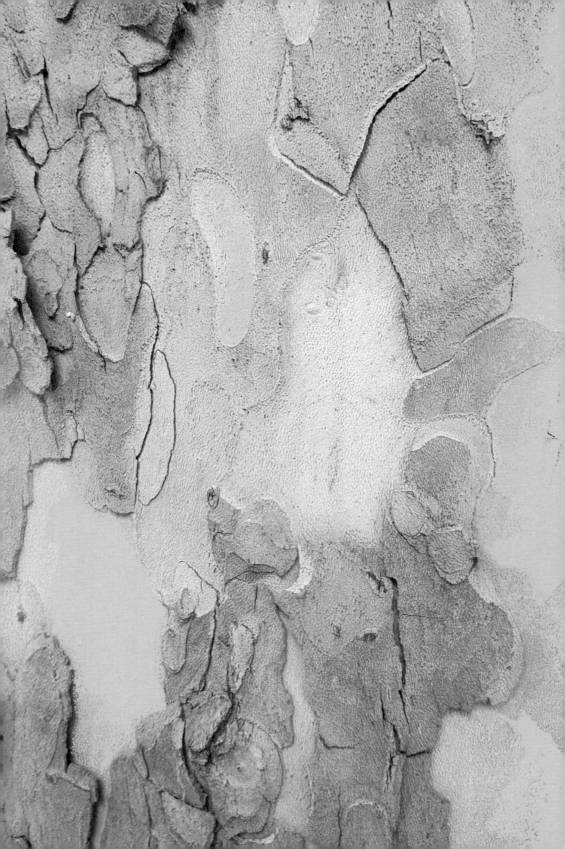

TREES
AS VICTIMS

IN ELWOOD I'VE come to know several generations of Sulphur-Crested Cockatoos (*Cacatua galerita*) who breed and roost in a Sugar Gum (*Eucalyptus cladocalyx*) next to Elster Creek and near the Sir John Monash Bridge. It's the tallest Eucalypt hereabouts. The birds are hilariously funny and loud, screeching around the neighbourhood, which irritates the other birds who dive bomb them, all to no avail because the cockies are so big and bold, they couldn't care less. There's a hole, several metres up in the tree, which is their nest. You can tell when it's inhabited due to the poo around the rim.

One spring morning, I hailed them. 'Hi, guys. What's happening?'

First one Cockatoo and then a second slowly raised their heads from the hole to look at me. Mum and Bub, most likely. They stared at me, curious and unafraid, and raised their crests in that comical manner which appears as if they're asking a question. They were clearly too high to be in any danger from me, the Earth's top predator. Then, with equal measure, they retreated into the tree.

The Sugar Gum is a meeting place for the Ravens (*Corvus coronoides*) who treat the Eucalypt as their conference centre. No, they're not Crows, even though both species are similar and belong to the Corvid family. Our Ravens are Indigenous. They're large birds whose iridescent black feathers gleam purple and green, and they strut around Elwood as if they own the joint.

Which, as far as Yaluk-ut Weelam mythology goes, they do. The god Waarn, who travels as a Crow (well, Raven), protects the waterways, the land on which I live and write. Bunjil, who travels as an Eagle, looks after everything else. However, there are no Wedge-Tailed Eagles (*Aquila audax*) in my neighbourhood. Probably a victim of the horrible habit that farmers practised decades ago of shooting them, believing them to be the killers of lambs. They weren't. Their prey was usually rabbits or perhaps dead or dying lambs. The Eagles were nearly wiped out in the process and, despite the fact they're now a protected species, they're still endangered.[1]

The Ravens regularly gather in the Sugar Gum's canopy and have what appears to be a parley of some sort (from which the word parliament derives). There must be around forty of them, communicating with one another in their harsh, distinctive voices. I watch them and wonder what they're saying to each other. Waarn would know, I imagine. And how do the Ravens reckon the appointed time at which to gather? Because they arrive en masse. They're not feeding, just perching and chatting for hours. It would be a delightful place to gather, in the Eucalypt's canopy, views stretching from Port Phillip Bay to the Dandenong Ranges, misty mauve in the distance. Breezy, too, but then birds know how to use their ally, the wind. Observe how birds navigate the skies on a gusty day. They're not afraid, they're revelling in it.

The Raven parliament was a sight with which the Yaluk-ut Weelam would have been familiar. The clan probably had Dreamings to explain it. It may have to do with seasonal change, or the ownership of territory, or the renewal of bonds among the Raven tribe, or the care of the land itself.

As Robyn Davidson writes, 'scholars are still trying to describe the "Dreaming" in such a way as to make it accessible to non-Aboriginal understanding'. Davidson describes it as 'a spiritual realm which saturates the visible world with meaning … a matrix of being … a parallel universe … a network of stories of mytho-logical heroes'.[2] At the time of creation, great ancestral beings moved across the land. As they fought and hunted, made love and gave birth, they transformed themselves from animal to human to animal once more. Their journeys and actions are inscribed on the landscape, concentrated in sacred sites such as trees and rivers. To Aboriginal people, 'the whole land is full of signs ... used and read ... as clearly as if it were bristling with notice-boards'.[3]

Over several days, I watched two Ravens build a nest in the European Ash on Elster Creek. It's only a short flight from the Sugar Gum. The couple chose the topmost branches to begin the tricky task of making the nursery, in the shape of a broad stick basket. First they had to organise the foundation: criss-crossing twigs and small branches in a dense but light construction. Too heavy it will fall, too sparse it won't take weight. Imagine making your home with your mouth; this will give you some idea of the process. The two of them worked as a team, and it must have been challenging but fun to combine on this important project with a new partner. Ravens pair for life and soon after they mate, they start nesting.

However, something went wrong. The birds disappeared, leaving the nest half finished. I'd walk past each day, speculating on where they were and what had transpired. So much can go awry in wild nature. Elwood is hardly 'wild', but it is for the Ravens. They don't depend on us—except for food scraps—and don't wish to have much to do with us. Like most birds, they want to get on with their lives and ignore us as much as possible. It's one of the most attractive features of birds: their independence from *Homo sapiens*, their commitment to their own communities. Dogs have had the wolfpack bred out of them to make them our devoted friends, while cats manage to have us at their beck and call while disdaining to give a glimmer of gratitude. Birds kept in captivity? To cage a creature born for the skies I find too awful to ponder.

A few weeks later, when I saw two Ravens near the nest I was thrilled. Had the original couple returned after illness or some other mishap? Would they take up where they had left off? But no, it was a new couple. They were looking to take over the nest as their own. They spent some time gazing at it and assessing the situation. Hmmm ... what to do? Is this a gift? Or an ill omen? They must have decided against it, because they never came back.

Months later, the skeleton of the nest remains, proving it was a good build after all.

I've never been much of a tree-hugger. Put it down to self-consciousness. Or squeamishness. Ants take a dim view of anyone or anything which interrupts their frantically busy passage. Or some other bug might take a fancy to my sensitive Celtic skin. But in 1999, on the day of Albert Tucker's funeral, I went and wrapped my arms around the Sugar Gum. Bert was a celebrated artist whom I'd known for more than two decades, whose biography I was then writing and at whose wake I was scheduled to speak. I was riddled with strong emotions and the tree—perhaps it was just my fancy—seemed to absorb them; when I let go of its broad, strong trunk my heart had ceased thundering and the buzz in my brain had settled. I was prepared for whatever the day offered.

Eucalypts can grow gigantically high, especially the Mountain Ash (*Eucalyptus regnans*), which made it a target for the colonial land clearers of the nineteenth century. It has the potential to reach 100 metres and its girth can exceed 20 metres. It can thrive for hundreds of years, which means looking at a mature Mountain Ash is truly to look back in time.

State Library Victoria has an excellent collection of prints and paintings which documents the relentless tree-felling mission of the colonialists. By telling the story of the landscape in graphic images, the artworks also create a narrative regarding the dispossession of Indigenous people, who may be seen as personifying the trees themselves as well as their fate. By the late nineteenth century, the felled tree stump had become an Australian national symbol for culture and sovereignty.

I'm not dismissing the necessity of felling trees to create roads and houses and paddocks, or the stalwart courage of the loggers themselves. It's the extremes to which some settlers went, the desire to gain control over nature at all costs, that same human hubris that relegates the status of the natural world and its creatures as inferior, part of a God-given system to be subjugated. It's a notion that goes all the way back to Genesis.

'Have dominion,' God advises Adam and Eve, 'over the fish of the sea, and over the birds of the air, and over the cattle and over all the earth, and over every creeping thing that creeps upon the earth.' To make the point clear, God says this not once but several times in Genesis 1:26–31. Do what you damn well like with nature, it's there to serve you. It's an attitude inimical to religious beliefs of many people, including First Nations, Hindus and Buddhists, whose own cultures have suffered as a result. I don't imagine Miranda Gibson would think much of it either.

Robert Bruce's engraving *Felling a Giant Gum Tree in the Ranges* (1869) is a disturbing image. In a lusciously rendered, ferny forest stands a huge tree which dwarfs the two woodcutters hacking into it. The men have built a small platform a few metres above the

Felling a Giant Gum Tree in the Ranges, 1869, Robert Bruce, engraving published in *Illustrated Australian news for home readers*, State Library Victoria.

ground and are presumably skilled enough to cut the tree in such a way that it won't fall on them. Bruce has dramatised the scene by casting the lower reaches of the tree in a kind of spotlight while the loggers swing their axes in rhythmic vigour. They are watched by a man on a horse and another fellow who seems to be quite well dressed, leaning on his cane—the property owner?

It reveals that even out there in the ranges (probably the Dandenong Ranges), settlement is taking place and gentlemen are making money from it. At the far left, in shadow, is another stump, signalling the ongoing logging process. The scale of the men against the tree makes it seem at first ludicrous that these puny humans could have the power to destroy such a grand and lovely thing. But that's the irony to which Bruce alludes in his melancholic homage to man and tree. As Don Watson observes, 'Nothing could match the sense of conquest that went with the axeman's labour in the primeval scrub.'[4]

Government equals 'civilisation' equals land clearance. Joseph Anderson Panton's *Government Residence, Melbourne 1837* (1880) centralises William Lonsdale's cottage as a symbol of newly established colonial authority.[5] In 1836, Lonsdale had been appointed police magistrate for Port Phillip District, a powerful position. Until Charles La Trobe was selected as superintendent three years later, Lonsdale was the law. It was he who decided the site for Melbourne. Lonsdale also chose the government 'Domain', seen here in Panton's work, as the site for Government House, which was built in 1876. Part of Lonsdale's role was to 'conciliate' with Aboriginal people.

In Panton's nostalgic evocation of early Melbourne, a group of Aboriginal people are seated on the ground and in conversation with three white men. All seem to be discussing boomerangs held by the white men. Is this a commercial transaction? Or an explanation by the Indigenous people of the boomerang's use? In the centre, Maude Lonsdale, Lonsdale's wife, feeds ducks and chickens. To the far right stands a tall Eucalypt against which lean discarded Aboriginal weapons, once used for hunting and warfare.

Government Residence, Melbourne 1837, 1880, Joseph Anderson Panton, oil on canvas, 59.4 × 89.9 cm, State Library Victoria.

While Panton's work includes Indigenous people, the idyllic depiction of relations between white and black ignores the devastation of habitat which signalled the latter's brutal banishment.

Thomas Clark's glowing vista *Emerald Hill and Sandridge from the Government Domain* (1857) takes its view across to Albert Park Lake. In the distance are the suburbs of Emerald Hill (now South Melbourne) and Sandridge (Port Melbourne).[6] It's a swathe of prime real estate. In the foreground, two loggers sit on a felled tree. A woman, presumably the wife of one, has arrived bringing lunch, accompanied by their child. Cattle, usurpers of traditional lands, graze nearby. Cast in golden light, it's meant to be a bucolic scene. Aboriginal people are not included, but they have an eerie presence, once again courtesy of a tall Eucalypt. It's a scar or canoe tree, which means a canoe or a shield was cut from its bark. It tells us that this tree was an important marker for Indigenous people as they walked through the country, like the Ngargee Tree at St Kilda Junction.

Clark, as you'll recall, painted Elwood's *Red Bluff, Elwood* (c.1860, National Gallery of Victoria).[7] Clark arrived in Melbourne

with his family around 1852. He'd had quite a successful career in England. He'd won a gold medal for landscape painting from the prestigious Royal Society of Arts, while in 1846 he was appointed head of Birmingham's School of Design. What attracted Clark to Victoria was probably the same lure attracting thousands from around the world—gold. Not that Clark set out for the Ballarat goldfields, but if he reckoned on being part of a prosperous burgeoning city, then he was right. 'Marvellous Melbourne', brimming with wealth, ambition and opportunity, was in the process of establishing itself.

Clark became a force in white Australia's first distinctive landscape painting movement, the Heidelberg School. In 1870, he was appointed drawing-master in the newly created School of Design which was part of the National Gallery. The very fact the school and gallery were founded indicates Victoria's cultural pre-eminence, its sense of itself as national leader in the arts, a role in which Melbourne still prides itself.

The school flourished under Clark's innovative guidance. Rather than insist students copy from works in the National Gallery collection, as did Eugene von Guérard, director of the painting school, Clark encouraged his students to sketch from nature. Two brilliant young artists, Tom Roberts and Fred McCubbin, were among Clark's students in 1875. Later, when they founded the artists' camps around Box Hill and Heidelberg where artists painted 'en plein air', it marked the beginning of a fresh, attentive attitude to the Australian landscape.

But am I reading Panton's and Clark's paintings correctly? As Bill Gammage points out, Aboriginal people were expert land carers. The terrain 'discovered' by white explorers and settlers was not necessarily 'wilderness': it was ordered and organised, subject to regular burning to keep the undergrowth sparse and to flush out animals for hunting purposes. What we see in these paintings may be what Indigenous people had created: the 'very pleasant and fertile' country where the trees were 'like plantations in a gentleman's park'.[8] Nonetheless these paintings provide the stage for the disappearance of Aboriginal people.

Photography brought the message home even more starkly. Michael J Drew's *Man with Large Uprooted Tree Stump* (1900) registers the bleak aftermath of clearing, while JC Flynn's *Mammoth Tree at Foster Gippsland* (c. 1906) offers a surreal solution to felling of old growth forest: a mammoth stump serves as home for man and horse. By then, the felled tree was such a national symbol it had become a photography studio prop.

In George Richards's carte de visite print *Ned Kelly the Bush-ranger* (c. 1880), Kelly and his rifle lean against a stump. In 1880, Kelly was hanged for the murders of three policemen. Yet Kelly, the celebrity outsider to lawful society, is depicted as a gentleman: his hair and beard are immaculately coiffed, he's fashionably clad and carrying a boater. The straw boater became popular around this time as a leisure wear item—the hat a chap wore on holidays or

Man with large uprooted tree stump, c. 1900, Michael J Drew, 12.2 × 16.5 cm, State Library Victoria.

Mammoth tree at Foster, Gippsland, c. 1906, J C Flynn, 9 × 6 cm, State Library Victoria.

while boating, hence the name. Kelly's left hand is the centralising point of the composition: Kelly wears a wedding ring though he never married.

George Richards has transformed Kelly into a gentleman and a husband, doing what a gentleman does: a spot of hunting and overseeing the clearing of his land. It's a curious image where Kelly, a reckless and desperate Irishman from an impoverished rural background, emanates the relaxed authority of an English lord. Richards's image presages the complex myths that arose about Kelly in Australian culture and which continue to resonate.

G. RICHARDS.   PHOTO.   BALLARAT.

Ned Kelly The Bushranger, c. 1870–1880, George Richards, 11 × 7 cm, State Library Victoria.

The convention of the tree stump as a symbolic prop is revisited more poignantly in nineteenth-century studio and outdoor photographs of Aboriginal people. Thomas John Washbourne's *Maggie Stone* (1870) shows a barefoot Indigenous girl, dressed in a European frock, her brow wreathed with leaves—a cruelly ironic touch given the wreath denotes victory. Maggie is seated on an arrangement of felled timber. Yet her confident pose is quite at odds with her expression which is so troubled, she looks close to tears.

Complete stillness was required of the subject for a nineteenth-century photograph so the image would not blur. Did that contribute to Maggie's unhappy gaze? It's difficult to ignore the photograph's context. Maggie is posed to represent a tree spirit, a dryad, a feminine emanation of place; a place, in fact, her people

Maggie Stone, 1870, Thomas John Washbourne, 9 × 6 cm, State Library Victoria.

had lost to the settlers. Most telling is the original title written on the back of the photograph: *Maggie Stone, Quadroon*, meaning she was a quarter-blood Aboriginal person, designating her as a racial specimen in colonial hierarchy.

John Hunter Kerr created the impressive but sad image *Group of Unidentified Aboriginal Men and Children from Framlingham Station* (c. 1865–75).[9] Framlingham was an Aboriginal reserve near the township of Warrnambool in south-western Victoria. In 1861, a request by the local Church of England to create the reserve was approved by the Aboriginal Protection Board, and by 1865, local Indigenous people were forced from their traditional lands to occupy the site. There were members of the Kirrae Wuurong clans and the Djargurd Wuurung people as well as the Gunditjmara people from Warrnambool.

In the photograph's timeframe, Framlingham was encountering turbulence. Firstly, local settlers were against the establishment of the reserve and petitioned the government to close it and use the property as farmland. Framlingham was briefly closed in the mid-1860s. But the Kirrae Wuurong people, now reconciled to staying there, had it successfully reopened. But it was not theirs to fully own: in those days, long before native title was awarded to Aboriginal people, much of the land was available for sale and it meant the size of the reserve shrank as the decades went by.

Worse was to come. Archie Roach's deservedly famous 1990 song *Took the Children Away* conveys what happened at Framlingham, and at many places across Australia. It is an anthem for 'the stolen generations', the children who were forcibly removed from their parents, and it captures the wrenching grief Aboriginal people experienced.

Roach's is a work of such wounded eloquence that, though I've heard it countless times, never fails to give me goosebumps as if my very skin is responding to the pain of which Roach sings. Roach presents the colonial custodians of Aboriginal people—the social workers and the police—who advise the families that they must understand why their children are being legally abducted.

The children will be taught 'how to really live', something which their parents are presumably unable to offer them. But learning the white man's way delivers a tragic irony: the children not only come to feel ashamed of themselves but they have been severed from the love and care of family as well as their land, culture and language. While Roach's father angrily tried to prevent his children being taken—Roach was four at the time—white might was stronger. *Took the Children Away* was the first song that Roach performed. It was a culmination of years of wandering, of drinking, of trying to locate relatives. The redemptive final words, 'the children came back', lifts the song's almost unbearable sadness into a realm where healing is possible.

In Kerr's study, the handsome band of bearded Aboriginal men has been posed either sitting on or standing against a large, felled tree. In front of them sit a group of six children. Their expressions are serious and attentive; there's no hint of amusement or boredom. The group direct their gaze with dignity at the photographer, giving the moment a sense of occasion.

Group of Aboriginal men and children from Framlingham station, all in European dress, c. 1865–1875, John Hunter Kerr, 13.8 × 20.1 cm, State Library Victoria.

John Hunter Kerr was a Scottish-born grazier who was also among Victoria's earliest amateur photographers. Frances Kerr wrote an account of her husband's time in Australia, *Glimpses of Life in Victoria*, published in 1872 under the pseudonym 'A Resident'.[10] In 1849, Kerr bought a property near Bendigo but it went broke, and Kerr moved to a property in north-west Victoria near the Loddon River. He had a low opinion of the local loggers whom he described as 'a lawless set'. Former convicts, they were also sly grog vendors who committed 'many outrages' (read rape) and lived 'wild irregular lives'.[11]

Kerr was fascinated by Aboriginal people. Of Kerr's thirty-seven photographs in the State Library, thirty-four are of Indigenous people. However, he subscribed to the prejudices of his day, viewing Aboriginal people as members of a 'doomed race'.[12] *Group of Unidentified Aboriginal Men and Children* is unusual in his oeuvre: most of his photographs show Aboriginal people living traditional lives on traditional lands—dressed in possum-skin cloaks, not wearing European clothes, or any clothes at all, carrying weapons, having a corroboree or seated cross-legged in a mia-mia, a temporary shelter made of bark, branches and leaves. They were the people whom Kerr knew from his local district, making them the Loddon and Murray Tribes, the Dja Dja Wurrung and Yorta Yorta people of the Kulin nation.

The Framlingham men do not look bowed: they have a powerful physical presence. For all their European clothes, they are warriors. If photography is a compact, however unconscious, between photographer and subject, Kerr reveals his respect and admiration for the men, and they return his tribute with gravitas. While Kerr's photograph indicates the problematic future for Aboriginal people under European rule, his other photographs document how some Indigenous people continued living a traditional life in the 1850s on the frontier. *Group of Unidentified Aboriginal Men* is haunting because it places the men near or on a felled tree, in a direct physical relation to lost lands and a way of life. It also captures a crucial historical juncture where the Framlingham people were trying to negotiate a new and viable future for their community, attempting to balance the black and the whitefella ways.

Indigenous artist Tommy McRae's vigorous and humorous pen and ink drawings counter the images of dispossession. In *Out Hunting for Dinner—A run of luck*, the trees are alive with a possum and goannas, game hunted by Aboriginal people. In *Lacland Black War Dancing*, a possum, perched on a branch, observes men, armed with boomerangs, spears and shields, engaged in a war dance. In McRae's image of nature, everything is imbued with the flow of energy. It shows differing approaches between European and Indigenous people: for the latter, the tree shares in and contributes to Aboriginal society.

While McRae also includes Europeans in some of his drawings, it's the reverse attitude to Panton's *Government Residence, Melbourne 1837*. In McRae's encyclopaedic view of his country, *Dancers with Weapons; Hunting and fishing; European house and couple*, a European couple observe a group of dancing Aboriginal men—they are the passive spectators to an energetic display of Indigenous culture which, given that the men are holding weapons, could be the preamble to, or the signification of, battle. An emu, who stands between the couple and the men, turns its head to look at the Europeans with curiosity, as if to say, 'What are you doing here?'

Like the Framlingham people, McRae also lived on a reserve, at Lake Moodemere, an idyllic lagoon near the Murray River town of Wahgunyah, now a wine-growing region. He was probably a member of the Kwatkwat people. McRae's first drawings were collected by the sculptor Theresa Walker at Barnawartha between 1861 and 1864 when McRae would have been around thirty.[13]

McRae was born, as far as can be deduced, at precisely the time that the colonial invasion of the upper Murray was beginning. The invasion gathered momentum around the middle of the nineteenth century, bringing successive waves of new occupants into the area whose activities destroyed much of the fabric of the traditional Aboriginal economy and culture. 'First came the pastoralists [squatters] with flocks of animals; then, in the 1850s,

Out hunting for dinner – a run of luck, c. 1865, Tommy McRae, pen and ink drawing, 21.8 × 27.8 cm, State Library Victoria.

Aboriginal Australian scenes and European people, 1862, Tommy McRae, pen and ink drawing, 21.8 × 27.8 cm, State Library Victoria.

came gold-diggers ... then came speculators, who became rich, or bankrupt, through enterprises such as riverboats and vineyards.'[14]

More tragic were the massacres. It was out on the frontier, distant from the capital and the bigger country towns, that the battles between white and black, and the slaughter of Aboriginal people, took place. As Lyndall Ryan reports, it is likely that more than a thousand Aboriginal people were killed in rural Victoria (then known as the Port Phillip District) between 1834 and 1859.[15]

McRae managed to rise to the challenges, and to make money— as a labourer, a stockman, a farmer and an artist, the last being his most financially lucrative career. A visitor to Lake Moodemere in 1886 described him as a 'man of substance' and as 'an astute financier, somewhat of a wag, and a draughtsman'.[16] By the time of McRae's death in 1901—coincidentally the year of Federation, when Australia became a nation—Wahgunyah's fortunes had declined. It was also surrounded by ring-barked but uncleared timber which presented 'a prospect ... rendered dreary by miles and miles of skeleton trees, with here and there a cultivated tree'.[17]

Ring-barking is a practice that slowly kills a tree: a thick ring of bark is cut from the trunk, thereby removing the phloem, the sap that provides sugars to the tree's roots. Unless it can be healed, the tree will inexorably starve to death above the wound. Ring-barking was a lazy way of land clearing: instead of all the muscle and sweat required to cut down a tree, it was a relatively easy process that, by and large, guaranteed the tree's death. It was as though some colonialists could not bear the sight of flourishing trees, any more than they could bear the sight of Aboriginal people, who were, in most cases, forcibly removed and condemned to a reserve, or as Lyndall Ryan's research indicates, murdered.

Unfortunately, ring-barking is a practice that has not gone out of fashion. In 2010 and again in 2013, Melbourne's historic Separation Tree was ring-barked by vandals in the Royal Botanic Gardens. It was one of the few trees in the gardens that predated colonisation. The 400-year-old River Red Gum (*Eucalyptus camaldulensis*), under which locals celebrated Victoria's separation from New South

Wales in 1850, was the subject of numerous grafting procedures, all of which failed. The culprits—and the reason for their act—have never been discovered.

On a chilly winter morning, gauzy with light rain, I went to visit the tree. From a distance, across a lawn that leads down to a lake, I could see, behind other foliage, three massive truncated branches, like fists raised angrily to the sky. I passed two garden workers, driving by in a golf buggy.

'Is that the Separation Tree?' I asked.

'Well, it was,' said the man ruefully.

When I rounded the bend and saw the tree full on, my first impulse was to weep. But it is such a grand being, and so very bold, even in death, that I repressed the urge. The vandals did their work well: the section they ring-barked is at least a metre wide and close to the ground, so they didn't build a platform like the loggers in *Felling a Giant Gum Tree in the Ranges*. They must have used chainsaws and worked at night.

Looking at the wound is to observe, up close, violent intent, cruelty and a sadistic delight in not only killing the tree but in shocking those who come to view it. Was it meant to be a sick joke? 'Separating' the Separation Tree? What remains is the trunk and several partly amputated branches. The canopy had to be removed because it could eventually fall and injure someone.

At the site, there's no information provided about what happened to the tree, which seems a shame, because its death is now part of its history, and of the gardens, too. I picked up a strip of its bark from the ground and put it in my pocket. A keepsake. It's in front of me on my desk as I write. It looks like a small abstracted sculpture of a bird in flight: there's the head and beak while the bark's fine wavey lines suggest gliding movement.

But all is not lost. As I walked away, I came across a young River Red Gum that was planted in 2001 to commemorate 150 years since the separation of Victoria from New South Wales. It is a seedling of the Separation Tree, its many times over grandchild, and it's healthy, and busy growing. Nature often finds a way.

Aboriginal people do not fell forests: they have been in the business of long-term conservation. From the time they arrived here, they used fire as 'one of the earliest and most efficient land management tools'.[18] As small groups of nomads travelled through the country, camping and hunting, they also burned the surrounding vegetation. As Scott Cane asks,

> How could people, as an immediate consideration, confront the threat of giant monitors, terrestrial crocodiles, giant snakes and lion-like possums concealed in the bush without wanting to do something about it? A positive and obvious step in their risk-management strategies would have been to burn—clear the scrub these animals lived in; burn the bush to expose the ground so both animals and their tracks could be seen; burn them; drive them from their burrows and lairs; remove their habitat.[19]

Aboriginal people leading traditional lives do so today. But they are keenly aware of the risks of wildfire and of the advantages they gain by managing it. They choose to burn in the cooler months, on lands some distance from their camp and with a significant gap, around five years, between burns. Firestick farming made 'the bush safe, it made it easier to access, it provided a means of communication, it improved hunting and gathering, and it encouraged productive regeneration'.[20] Europeans have learned this skill from Indigenous people and it is now regarded as a necessary deterrent to the occurrence of summer fires in Australia where the dry Eucalypt forests can ignite with roaring intensity.

However, our summer blazes are not always caused by nature; some are the deliberate acts of humans who apparently get a thrill from seeing a forest burn and who cause not only havoc and devastation, but the injuries or deaths of people and animals, together with placing at risk the firefighters who try to quell the blaze.

Kathryn Collins of the University of Wollongong's Centre for Environmental Risk Management of Bushfires, together with her colleagues, published a report based on data on more than 113 000 bushfires between 1997 and 2009 across New South Wales and Victoria. Of the fires with a known cause, 47 per cent were accidental—cigarettes, escaped burn-offs and campfires, or sparks from equipment or powerlines, while 13 per cent were from lightning strikes. Forty per cent were deliberately lit.[21]

Chloe Hooper's gripping narrative *The Arsonist: A mind on fire* navigates the inner world of Brendan Sokaluk. A bitter, vengeful loner, Sokaluk started dreadful fires in Victoria's Latrobe Valley in 2009, which were later known as Black Saturday. Ten people died, as did thousands of animals, more than 150 homes were razed and 36 000 hectares burned. Sokaluk was a Country Fire Authority volunteer. At trial, the jury heard he was bullied at school. He had autism and an intellectual disability. He was sentenced to nearly eighteen years jail and could be released in 2026. After her exhaustive research, Hooper remains baffled by Sokaluk and what motivated him. Why he lit the fires is 'the impossible question'.[22]

I wonder if it's the same mentality of the Separation Tree vandals, and the arsonists of Miranda Gibson's Tasmanian valley, writ large and deadly.

WOMEN OF
THE BANYAN

As I write, it's mid-May 2020 and I'm concerned for the women of Varanasi. The time is approaching for an annual, sacred, women-only ritual in northern India, which this year falls on 22 May. But it's unlikely to take place because the entire planet is in the thrall of COVID-19. From *The Times of India*, I learn there are eighty-seven people afflicted in Varanasi and the city is shuttered.

Around the world, millions are infected and thousands have died. Most of us are frightened and anxious. We watch the news all day long. We're obliged to stay in our homes and keep a 1.5-metre distance from others in the street or in the supermarket, even when walking through Elwood's pleasant greenery. Shops close. There's little traffic. The quiet is spooky. The global economy is teetering and only a lunatic like Donald Trump believes we'll come out of this okay.

In Varanasi, the women are praying. They're asking the goddess Savitri to grant Varanasi respite from the pandemic so they can honour her. Each year, married women gather to cast a spell for their husbands' longevity. The ceremony isn't celebrated in a temple: it takes place beneath a Banyan.

Situated on the Ganges, Varanasi is India's most holy and most visited pilgrimage site. There are literally hundreds of temples, as well as the presence of the great goddess herself, Ganga Maiya (Mother Ganges). But COVID-19 is crippling Varanasi's spiritual industry. The ritual of bathing in the Ganges, to literally wash away one's sins, is forbidden. The business of publicly cremating the dead in funeral pyres along the Ganges has more or less ceased. So has the tree-felling industry (mainly from Himalayan forests) that supports it. Each pyre uses between 200 to 400 kilos of wood, and usually Varanasi burns through about 80 tonnes per day. The cremations take place continuously and are a huge draw both for the faithful and the merely curious. 'Varanasi is the India of your imagination,' declares a travel website.[1] For the time being, the smoke and the stink of burning flesh has evaporated. But then so have the jobs of those who cater for the cremations, the men from a special caste known as the Doms.

They survive from the benevolence of the families who book this service, which can cost anywhere from $20 to $70, depending on the cremation package. Not exorbitant for a funeral but for many struggling Indian families, quite steep. Transporting a dying family member through the mayhem, noise and squalor that is Varanasi is challenging enough. The narrow alleys of the old city are thick with people, rickshaws, sacred cows, food stalls, shops and zooming, honking motor bikes. Towering above the river and the ghats, or tiered embankments, rise palaces, ashrams, crumbling houses, ornate temples and haphazardly built dwellings. The terminally ill flock there. Some reside at a basic hospice, known as the Death Hostel, where they are cared for until they pass away. Each week several hundred corpses arrive by train. For devout Hindus, cremation at Varanasi offers *moksha* (salvation), an escape from the endless cycle of birth and rebirth. Varanasi is a dramatic public space consecrated to the enactment of dying.

The Banyan or Bengal Fig is India's national tree and is highly regarded across Asia. You'll recall it's the staunch architectural prop for the homes of the Korowai in Indonesia. The Korowai, like many Australian Indigenous people, are animists: they feel intrinsically connected to the Earth which is alive with spirits, of both the kind and the cruel variety, making the entire planet, its forests, mountains, seas and rivers, and all of its critters, if not sacred, then imbued with a religious significance. However, from around the ninth to the thirteenth centuries, most of Indonesia gradually converted to Islam. With a Muslim population of around 202 million, Indonesia is the largest of all Muslim nations. Like Christianity, Islam is monotheistic, so while the Banyan is treated with respect, and it forms part of the nation's emblem—signifying strength and growth—it's not worshipped.

Hinduism, however, with its crowded pantheon of gods, retains its veneration for the Banyan, which like all sacred trees in India, is believed to be a powerful animate being. More than that, it's considered to be immortal. That's due to its ability to self-propagate. The Banyan grows long aerial roots which sprout from the higher, thicker branches and which, in the words of poet Robert Southey, 'plummet … towards the ground'. He continues,

> So like a temple did it seem that there
> A pious heart's first impulse would be prayer.[2]

Which is precisely how the women of Varanasi regard it.

Over the course of time the roots become massive trunks, so that a single tree can create a small forest radiating steadily outward from the original trunk. Its sheer scale, capacious shade and ability to flourish in the harshest conditions make it a potent symbol. As David Haberman notes, the Banyan 'can reproduce itself and extend itself into time endlessly by creating new and self-supporting trunks'.[3]

Many Hindu deities are associated with trees, which are included in the myths and rites for that god. For the Banyan, it's Yama, a slightly scary fellow, because he's similar to the Greek Hades, lord of death and the underworld. It is he who will come for you at the hour of your demise. Thus the Banyan is often planted near cemeteries, symbolising Yama's direct relationship with the dead.

The story of Yama and the Banyan arose due to Savitri, the enterprising wife of Satyavan. Savitri was a princess who was not only formidably smart but tall and attractive as well. So intimidating was she that no suitor dared approach her. Savitri decided to find her own match and, after consulting her parents, set off across the countryside in a golden chariot. Her choice fell on the handsome young woodcutter Satyavan. In a classic trope of the fairy tale, Satyavan was actually a prince who'd fallen on hard times. Savitri was undeterred by his lowly status—indicating her romantic idealism—as well as by the awful news that Satyavan had been cursed to die in one year's time.

As the day neared, Savitri fasted and meditated to spiritually prepare herself for the rigours ahead. Then the couple withdrew to the forest where they sheltered beneath a Banyan. Satyavan was growing progressively weak and ill, and he rested his head on Savitri's lap. Suddenly a being 'as radiant as the sun appeared; he was dark in color, wearing a crown, and dressed in yellow clothing'.[4] It was Yama, come to claim Satyavan's soul and escort him to the underworld. Savitri thought fast: first, she prayed to the Banyan to protect Satyavan's body, then she went after Yama and her husband's soul, which Yama had tied with a leash.

Boldly, Savitri engaged in a question-and-answer game with Yama. It's a favourite 'detective' device employed in myth to heighten tension and to reveal the strengths or failings of the protagonists. Think of Oedipus and the Sphinx. Yama was so impressed by Savitri's devotion and her willingness to literally go to hell for her husband, that he told her he would grant her several boons—except one: she could not ask for her husband's life. Savitri asked that Satyavan and his family be restored to their former royal status. Her next wish was to bear one hundred sons. As soon as Yama agreed, he realised that Savitri had outwitted him: for Savitri to be pregnant her husband must be alive and well. Yama, however, proved to be a good loser and gave Satyavan back his life.

I don't know if Savitri gave birth to one hundred sons—a dismal request indicating the inferior status of girls in Indian society—but she is treated as a goddess, a deity representing love, loyalty and fecundity. Though Savitri's story is a minor episode in the epic Sanskrit poem the *Mahabarata*, it has earned Savitri ongoing worship among married women who have designed a ceremony to secure her favour.

At the new moon in the month of May, women ready themselves for the day-long puja (act of worship). They have already been fasting. A ritual morning bath—for purification—is followed by attiring themselves in their most vividly coloured saris. Some like to don their lavish red wedding saris, emphasising their connection with Savitri, the good wife.

In 2007, David Haberman, professor of religious studies at Indiana University, attended several pujas for Savitri in Varanasi. The ceremony begins at dawn. On the day of one ceremony, Haberman says the weather was 'unusually cool and pleasant for mid-May on the plains of northern India; the sky was cloudy and a light rain had just ended'. The women were 'already busy in the dim morning light making their offerings to the goddess …

Women performing Banyan ritual, Bhopal, Prakash Singh/AFP. 2020.

worshipping the banyan tree, and wrapping it with string'.[5] The Banyans are found in the city's streets, so they are not vast specimens, but growing as best they can in confined spaces. Somehow it makes the ritual even more touching: the women perform the ceremony in their own neighbourhood, transforming a busy urban environment into a sacred site.

One woman showed Haberman her puja basket containing presents for the goddess: water from the Ganges, turmeric paste, cooked chickpeas, sweets, puffed bread, balls of cooked wholemeal flour, a jasmine garland, marigold flowers and sindoor powder. The latter is vermilion, a dense opaque pigment with a clear, brilliant red hue. Married women apply it to the part in their hair and a dot between their eyebrows known as a bindi, denoting sexual energy and fertility. The woman also showed Haberman 'two tender fig buds from a banyan tree that she intended to eat to break her fast right after she finished her worship'.[6]

Each gathering can involve hundreds of women. Worshippers approach the tree, placing their gifts of flowers and food around it, and pray to Savitri to grant longevity to their husbands. Then, taking red and yellow string, symbolic of marriage and good fortune, the women slowly circle the Banyan in single file, wrapping its trunk many times over. The identities of Savitri and the Banyan merge so the tree becomes the body of the goddess, which the women stroke affectionately.

It's Friday 22 May and I'm searching the internet for reports of Savitri celebrations in Varanasi. The city is about four hours behind Melbourne, so it's 6 a.m. there, and the women would be up and about performing their puja. *The Times of India* gives no information about the local government relaxing shutdown restrictions, so perhaps the women will somehow celebrate the festival at home this year. Or not at all. But what, I hear you asking rather impatiently, does that matter?

It's just that I feel I'm missing something. It has to do with the binding of the Banyan. The very word means control, legally, an obligation that cannot be broken. Indian mythologist Devdutt Pattanaik describes the binding as 'imitative magic: by symbolically going around the immortal tree, the women are binding immortality into their married life'.[7] The binding is at the core of the ritual, where the women unite in a sisterhood of prayer, murmuring invocations to the goddess. After the ceremony, the Banyan looks as though it has been exquisitely embroidered in bright colours, enhancing the tree's aesthetic, and its powerful presence.

The only way to make a spell work is to *believe*. If it were me, if I were binding the Banyan, what would I wish for? Savitri bargained for her husband's life, his family's good fortune and her own fertility. And won. In myth, that translates as eternity. Immortality.

Then I find it, the synchronicity, that moment as writers we can never predict but earnestly desire. 'City of Widows: The 38,000 forgotten women of Varanasi.'[8] Before I click on the article, I see an accompanying photograph of a hauntingly beautiful, elderly woman, clad in a white sari, sitting on a pavement, her hands outstretched to beg. She's skeletally thin and, as she gazes into the camera, her eyes are dark pools of misery.

I learn that to be a widow in India is the worst of all possible catastrophes. The widow is a living example of bad luck. As Pattanaik comments, 'in traditional Indian society, a woman's chastity and fidelity ensured the longevity of her husband's life. If she became a widow, it was because she wasn't chaste enough. This was one of the reasons given for the practice of sati, in which a widow immolated herself on her husband's funeral pyre to prove her fidelity to her dead husband.'[9]

While sati has long been outlawed, thanks to England's imperial might in the nineteenth century, it may seem a better choice than the existence the widows are forced to endure. There would be the terrifying moments of agony and asphyxiation on the pyre compared to a life of poverty and exclusion, where the most the widow can hope for is to die—soon. She prays for it daily. The reason so many widows gather in Varanasi is the same reason that the dying congregate there: it's a sacred city and to die in its environs provides liberation from rebirth.

A widow's fate unfolds like this. Once her husband dies, the family turns on her. She is made to shave her head, then don a white sari, the colour of mourning, which she is expected to observe for the rest of her life. It makes her, literally, a pariah. She's then kicked out of her home, usually by her mother-in-law, and abandoned by her relatives. Violence, sometimes death, can accompany those episodes. The women rarely have a saleable skill, let alone an education. Older women go into the streets to beg. Younger widows are often pressured into prostitution. It's regarded as sacrilegious to remarry. Anyway, what man would choose a woman who had caused her husband's death? The widows usually reside in ashrams, which are also tourist destinations where visitors can gawk at these tragic creatures or, more helpfully, offer donations to keep the ashrams going. Even the ashrams are suspect. As N Narasimhan points out, while they are 'ostensibly run to protect widows', in reality they 'treat young widows as cash cows'.[10]

When Toronto-based Deepa Mehta decided to make a film about the Varanasi widows, she learned how aggressive and inflexible were the conservative religious and government forces behind their treatment. In 2000, Mehta was about to start shooting *Water*, the last in her critically acclaimed Elements trilogy, the other films being *Fire* (1996) and *Earth* (1998). The water in the title is the Ganges and Mehta's main production base was constructed on the ghats.

A severe censorship system operates in India. Before foreign films can be shot, directors must submit scripts and all production details to the government. If a film is approved, the government appoints a special liaison officer with wide powers to monitor all aspects of the production. Though Mehta had secured approval, it was withdrawn the day before shooting was to commence.

The following day about five hundred demonstrators—an alliance of Hindu fundamentalist groups—marched to the Ganges where they burned the sets and threw the remains into the river. The police did not intervene.[11] Fortunately, Mehta and David Hamilton, her husband and the film's producer, were absent that day. So it was by sheer chance that Mehta and Hamilton hadn't come face to face with the rioters. Mehta's effigy was burned and she was accused of being anti-Hindu. Hamilton comments, 'Even though I don't think that there was an intent to cause us any bodily harm, we were under death threat.'[12]

As Mehta continued to desperately negotiate with the government, the film's finances dwindled. The cast and crew agreed to work without pay. High profile artists such as musician Ravi Shankar publicly supported Mehta but it did not sway the resolve of the right-wing forces. When the nearby state of Madhya Pradesh offered to host the film, Uma Bharti, a female politician, told the press that Mehta and her crew 'would be stoned' if they attempted to make the film, while Mahant Shankara, president of a Hindu extremist group, declared, 'We can go to any extent, even sacrifice our lives and take others' lives to stop this film.'[13] Mehta had no recourse but to shut down production.

But this is a story with a good outcome, at least for Mehta. At first, she was so angered and demoralised by the film's demise she could not consider returning to it. Then, in 2005, the project was revived and Sri Lanka was selected for *Water's* location. Mehta reflects, 'Now that the film is complete, I can look back on the journey it has taken to make it ... The anguish, the death threats, the politics, the ugly face of religious fundamentalism—we experienced them all. Has it been worth it? I often wonder.'[14] But Mehta must have been heartened by *Water's* reception: it was widely praised and nominated for several international awards, including the 2007 Academy Award for Best Foreign Language Film. That year it was also released in India with an 'unrestricted' rating.

Mehta focused on three widows: a bubbly, strong-willed eight-year-old girl, Chuyia (Sarala Kariyawasam); a sensitive and attractive young woman, Kalyani (Lisa Ray); and Shakuntala (Seema Biswas), an embittered, older woman. While the film is set in 1938, child marriage remains a feature of Hindu life. India has the highest number of child marriages in the world. For many Hindus, women are regarded as property, and not especially valuable property at that. Dispatching female children as quickly as possible is often paramount in poor homes.

At an ashram run by the unscrupulous Madhumati (Manorama), the three widows become friends. Kalyani is forced into prostitution, a situation which leads to her suicide. Madhumati then designates Chuyia to take Kalyani's place. Shakuntala tries to save Chuyia. But it's too late and, when she finds Chuyia, the child is traumatised and insensate. Shakuntala carries Chuyia to the train station where Mahatma Gandhi is addressing the crowds. She has heard that Gandhi advocates remarriage for all young widows.

Shakuntala sees Narayan (John Abrahams) on the train. A young lawyer from the upper Brahmin caste, he'd fallen in love with Kalyani. Despite his family's opposition, Narayan had been determined to marry her. Kalyani took her life when she discovered her client was Narayan's father. When Narayan confronts him, the older man is cynical and unabashed, advising his son, 'So you know she's not a goddess. Don't marry her. Keep her as a mistress.'

Narayan's father is the same man who rapes Chuyia. Perhaps the film's most unnerving scene is where Chuyia, blithely ignorant of her fate, is led to a darkened bedroom, announcing, 'I'm here to play.'

Devastated by Kalyani's death, Narayan decides to leave his home and family. Narayan is a devoted follower of Gandhi's. At the station, Narayan sees Chuyia and Shakuntala in the crowd. As the train departs, Shakuntala shoves Chuyia into Narayan's arms. 'Take her to Gandhi!' cries Shakuntala.

Did the widows of Varanasi see it? Or the daughters of Savitri? Because the true meaning behind the binding of the Banyan is fear. The women who perform the rite know what awaits them if their husband predeceases them. They've seen the widows begging in the streets. They're aware of the ashrams. Also, the future of young widows. What an uneasy existence for a woman, trying to fulfil the role of the good wife, tenderly and anxiously caring for her husband, knowing that on his longevity depends her comfort and security, perhaps even her life!

There is some hope, though, for the widows of Varanasi. Lord Raj Loomba is a member of the British House of Lords. On 23 June 2005, he launched International Widows' Day which has been officially recognised by the United Nations. The date has a special poignancy for Loomba. It was the day his father died and his mother's life changed immediately. Loomba's grandmother, herself a widow, harassed his mother, forcing her to shave her head and to adopt a white sari.

At Loomba's wedding, the officiating priest told his mother to move away from the altar in case she brought bad luck to the new couple. 'That really made me angry,' Loomba recalls. 'I thought how could a mother who gave birth to me, educated me, looked after me, who always wished me well—how could she cause problems for me?'[15] It led him to start the Loomba Foundation, which promotes the economic empowerment and welfare of disadvantaged widows and their children—teaching them computer or sewing skills or educating them as teachers or engineers, therefore attempting to end the cycle of poverty, misery and ignorance.

A binding is a spell designed to prevent something bad happening. Control events. Determine outcomes. It needs to be repeated in order to maintain its efficacy. It's why in 2020 the married women of Varanasi completed the ritual in their homes, using sticks of fragrant Sandalwood (*Santalum album*) to symbolically replace the Banyan.[16] Binding invokes the power which the wives yearn to wield, not only to protect their husbands, but also themselves from those who are closest and most dangerous to them—their mothers or mothers-in-law. Hoping to placate them. Enlist their sympathy. Mother, do not abandon me. Savitri, save me. The tree is the omnipotent feminine that can safeguard and assist, or sentence the supplicant to a life of suffering.

What is a spell? Isn't it just a prayer solemnly enacted?

If I believed in prayer, I would pray for the women of the Banyan.

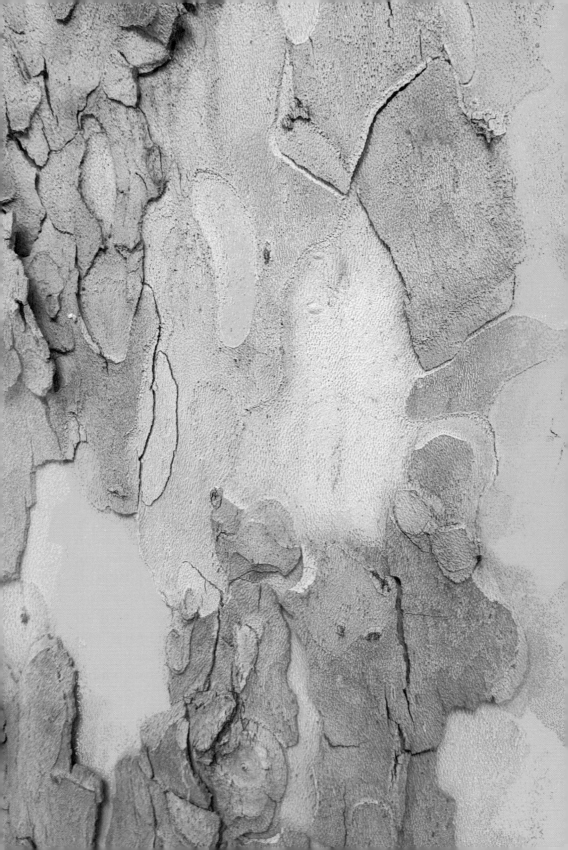

FAIRY-TALE
FORESTS

I'M IN A forest in an art gallery. It's a labyrinth made of drifting voile curtains in subtle tones of mauve and grey imprinted with towering, dark images of trees. It reaches from a very high ceiling to the floor. Though it's in a public place, this forest makes me feel sequestered. It's shadowy and somehow secret. What's around the next corner? Mystery? Revelation? A nasty surprise? I think of Little Red Riding Hood and the other fairy-tale children whose exploration of the forest can symbolise maturity, courage and independence. The trek into the unconscious, the reward of self-knowledge, is a process Bruno Bettelheim described as 'the uses of enchantment'.[1]

I follow the circular path, past the tree-curtains which move gently in the breeze created by my wake. The labyrinth is composed of three concentric rings like those of a tree. Trees are, in fact, giant organic recording devices that contain, in their rings, 'information about past climates, civilisations, ecosystems and even galactic events, much of it many thousands of years old'.[2] In recent times, the techniques for extracting information from tree rings—dendrochronology—have been honed and expanded.[3] As more tree data becomes available, a much richer perspective emerges of life on Earth. Trees tell stories about time, time shared between us and them. It's something we often don't realise or acknowledge, our communal past with plants. As if the only history was human history, recorded by us, the winners in the biological gambling game,

the ones who seem to control the Earth, the ones who believe they
rule nature.

I continue to walk through this forest of perpetual twilight, with
its shades of indigo and shimmering silver. It feels like a place of
contemplation, even mourning. A precious place. There is beauty
here but also sadness. Both the trees' strength and delicacy are
palpable: their vast bodies dwarf me yet are rendered fragile and
ghostly by the soft-hued, diaphanous veils. Nature's contradictions
are presented: it's tough but vulnerable, resistant but defenceless,
surviving but teetering on the brink of collapse. Truths we ignore
at our peril and which are constantly being played out across
our planet.

I don't want to leave the labyrinth. I want to stay here and learn.
Ordinary life seems faraway, while the symbolic life, the journey
offered by the art-forest, reminds me of one of nature's greatest
gifts—its ability to inspire humans, to *teach* us.

Forest: Theatre of trees (2018–19) is a sculptural installation by
Janet Laurence that accompanied her retrospective at Sydney's
Museum of Contemporary Art Australia in 2019. As curator Rachel
Kent notes, 'Trees have been a fixture of Laurence's art since the
beginning of her career' in the early 1980s.[4] Laurence comments,

> I've had a deep environmental consciousness for as long as I can
> remember. Trees factor into that consciousness, so I also look
> at the loss of forests and the enormity of that for our planet. I
> look at trees with enormous wonder and joy, but at the same
> time, the realisation that they are gravely threatened. There is
> the feeling of *this can't last*.[5]

Existing in a visual spectrum between art, science, imagination and
memory, Laurence's *Forest* is a kind of organic architecture that
reveals and underscores our relationship with nature. Conscious of
ecology, Laurence addresses global environmental catastrophe, and
the war against nature, waged by governments and corporations all
over the world.

Forest (Theatre of Trees), 2018–19, installation view, *Janet Laurence: After Nature*, Museum of Contemporary Art Australia, Sydney, 2019, dye sublimation print on voile, aluminium extrusion, mesh, tulle, painted leaves, archival scientific images. Collection of the artist, image courtesy the Museum of Contemporary Art Australia. © the artist, photograph: Jacquie Manning.

One example is Brazil's Amazon rainforest, imperilled by right-wing president Jair Bolsonaro. In 2019, he vowed to open the forest to industry and scale back its protections, and, as Matt Sendy reports, 'his government has followed through, cutting funds and staffing to weaken the enforcement of environmental laws. In the absence of federal agents, waves of loggers, ranchers and miners moved in, emboldened by the president and eager to satisfy global demand.'[6]

While Bolsonaro's government has made some concessions to combat illegal clear-cutting, the president has reaffirmed his long-standing position of disdain towards conservation work. He once said that Brazil's environmental policy was 'suffocating the country'; he vowed on the campaign trail that not 'a square centimetre' of land would be designated for Indigenous people; and in November 2019, he brushed aside official data about deforestation.[7]

By June 2020, the COVID-19 outbreak only made the situation worse. The number of deaths and infections soared as the country's medical system struggled to deal with the rate of the illness, the sheer numbers of people requiring care and protection or, in many cases, burial. Brazil's figures were among the highest of any country in the world. It was worse than the country's experience of the 1918 flu pandemic. Meanwhile illegal loggers, miners and land grabbers cleared swathes of the Amazon with impunity as law enforcement efforts were hobbled by the pandemic.

The razed areas will almost certainly make way for a rash of fires even more widespread and devastating than the ones in 2019.[8] The newly cleared patches are typically set ablaze during the drier months of August to October to prepare the land for cattle grazing, often spiralling out of control into wildfires. The return for beef cattle exports hovers around $5 billion for Brazil which is, after the production of soya beans, its most lucrative trade item.

From January to April 2020, an estimated 120175 hectares of Amazon tree cover was slashed, a 55 per cent increase from the same period in 2019 and an area roughly twenty times the size of Manhattan, according to Brazil's National Institute for Space Research, a government agency that tracks deforestation with satellite images.[9]

Such figures make it easy to feel demoralised. Helpless. Shakespeare wrote,

> How with this rage shall beauty hold a plea,
> Whose action is no stronger than a flower?

Laurence offers an eloquent protest against this tsunami of dis-respect towards nature—the unbridled and wilful destruction of trees and plants and rivers and creatures and oceans. She poetically calls attention to the plight of the natural world. To be an advocate, a supporter, a humble and present audience to the fate of living things. To be on the *side* of nature, in the war *against* nature.

Laurence engages with re-making the environment through attentive, inventive care, bringing nature within the scope of the gallery and its audience. Configuring what Laurence describes as a place of 'revival and resuscitation', she appeals to our sense of responsibility and agency in re-mediating the natural world, connecting an aesthetics of care to an aesthetics of cure.[10] She comments, 'My works attempt to create a reflective space for memory. It is a space in which one lingers so that one's memory is activated. It's what I call a "slow space".'[11] That was an alluring aspect of her installation, its ability to engage the viewer viscerally. A remarkable feat—to slow time down. Perhaps it was why I resisted leaving.

Laurence's intention is to heal nature, which makes *Theatre of Trees* not merely an elegy for the natural world but for a vibrant connection between the artist, the trees and us, the audience. *Theatre of Trees* can be viewed as a site of mourning undoubtedly— lamentations for the devastating loss that humans have wrought on forests—but in the act of representing loss, Laurence models ways in which we might enable what remains to flourish, especially to flourish as hope in our hearts.

What did I learn from my journey into Laurence's forest? Did I emerge wiser or stronger like a fairy-tale child?

Entering the forest is an evocative image in fairy tales, symbolising a rite of passage and a hero journey. Since 1812, when German writers Jacob and Wilhelm Grimm published the first volume of their *Kinder und Hausmärchen* (*Children's and Household Tales*), the stories have captured the imaginations of children and adults alike. Characters such as Little Red Riding Hood, Hansel and Gretel, Cinderella and Snow White are embedded in Western culture, their stories supplying resonant and compelling narratives of innocence, fear, loss and triumph over adversity. Many of these tales were originally published in 1697 in volumes by Charles Perrault and Marie-Catherine Le Jumel de Barneville, Baroness d'Aulnoy, the latter responsible for coining the term 'fairy tale'.[12] It's a name that's stuck, despite the fact that fairies rarely make an appearance. The stories were reworked and further popularised by the Brothers Grimm.

A central motif is the forest journey. When Little Red Riding Hood sets off to visit Grandma, she's firmly warned by her mother not to stray from the path. Mama seems to know her daughter's predilection for wandering. Entering the forest, Red Riding Hood meets the Wolf. She's so innocent that she's unafraid of him and they have quite a pleasant exchange as the Wolf gleans information from her about the location of Grandma's cottage. The Wolf suggests Red Riding Hood chill out. Take a ramble through the woods. Pick some flowers and listen to birdsong, and she complies. After a while, she remembers her task: she must deliver wine and a freshly baked cake to her grandmother who is ill. The Wolf, however, has arrived before her and swallowed Grandma whole.

When Little Red Riding Hood arrives at the house, she feels strangely uneasy, reflecting that usually she enjoyed spending time with her grandmother. She stands by Grandma's bed where the famous dialogue ensues.

> 'Oh! grandmother, what big ears you have!'
> 'All the better to hear you with, my child.'
> 'But, grandmother, what big eyes you have!'
> 'The better to see you with, my dear.'
> 'But, grandmother, what large hands you have!'
> 'All the better to hug you with.'
> 'Oh! But, grandmother, what terrible big teeth you have!'
> 'All the better to eat you with!'

Gustave Doré's *Little Red Riding Hood* (c. 1862, National Gallery of Victoria) emphasises the drama of the moment by picturing the girl in bed with the Wolf.[13] It's an unsettling scene. The Wolf is wearing Grandma's mob-cap, with its lace fringe and green bow, pulled down to disguise his face. Red Riding Hood has removed

Little Red Riding Hood. c.1862, Gustave Doré, National Gallery of Victoria, Melbourne, Gift of Mrs S Horne, 1962. This digital record has been made available on NGV Collection Online through the generous support of Digitisation Champion Ms Carol Grigor through Metal Manufactures Limited.

her cloak but wears a signature red cap. She gazes at the Wolf with a mixture of fascination and fear. It's a weird, intimate moment which Doré captures well. Surely the girl can see the beast's snout? His claws? Can she not apprehend the danger? Why doesn't she run for her life?

Then Little Red Riding Hood is also consumed. But that's not the end of the story, at least as far as the Brothers Grimm were concerned. To make sure there's a consoling finale they introduce another character, the hunter. Passing by the house, the hunter hears snoring. He thinks it's Grandma and decides to check up on her. He finds the Wolf asleep in bed, his appetite sated. Rather than shoot the Wolf, the hunter, concerned that the girl and her grandmother might be alive inside him, takes scissors and slits the beast open. Lo and behold, Little Red Riding Hood and Grandma emerge unscathed. Red Riding Hood declares, 'How dark it was inside the wolf!' As Bruno Bettelheim comments, 'a charming, "innocent" young girl swallowed by a wolf is an image which impresses itself indelibly on the mind'.[14]

Like millions of children, I adored the Brothers Grimm. Bettelheim makes the point that the stories are satisfying because justice is meted out, so while some tales are violent, for the child they make perfect sense. The behaviour of adults can seem unfair to the child, who is smaller and weaker than the big, powerful people—like mothers and grandmothers—who rule her world. To see wicked, older folk punished—like the murderous stepmother in *Sleeping Beauty* who is forced to dance in shoes of red-hot iron until she dies—is gratifying indeed.

Also, I longed to have adventures and the Brothers Grimm present an array of fantastic, terrifying and rewarding quests not only for children but for girls in particular. Some of the most enduring tales—*Sleeping Beauty, Snow White, Beauty and the Beast, Rapunzel*—feature female protagonists. Even when a boy is involved, he often takes a lesser role. Turned out of their home by their stepmother, Hansel and his younger sister Gretel are condemned to wander the forest. In its depths, they discover a delicious house made of bread and cakes and sugar. It's a lure belonging to a witch who captures the children. She's a cannibal who plans to eat them both. But Gretel gets the better of her. Gretel tricks the witch into climbing into the oven to test its temperature. Then she slams shut the door and the witch is roasted alive. Gretel is also the one who navigates the return path to their father's home, their stepmother having conveniently died.

The Brothers Grimm's stories provide the voyage into the unknown. They set my imagination on fire, and I still regard them fondly, and with gratitude. Dear Jacob and Wilhelm, thank you for encouraging me to set my cap at fate. For suggesting I cast myself as the heroine in my own adventures. For alerting me to the helpful (and not so helpful) creatures—witches, wolves, ducks and dwarves—I may encounter on my travels. To move between the worlds of imagination and reality, without losing a foothold in either. For providing a 'happy ending' which, despite its wishful thinking, strikes a comforting note.

Bettelheim's passionate defence of fairy tales in *The Uses of Enchantment: The meaning and importance of fairy tales* (1976) re-popularised the stories. His psychoanalytic emphasis refreshed the tales for a 1970s audience, though Bettelheim caught the tales' grace and element of surprise without becoming too technical about Freudian interpretations. He wrote,

> Through the centuries (if not millennia) during which, in their retelling, fairy tales became ever more refined, they came to convey at the same time overt and covert meanings—came to speak simultaneously to all levels of the human personality, communicating in a manner which reaches the uneducated mind of the child as well as that of the sophisticated adult.[15]

Bettelheim's reading of *Little Red Riding Hood* locates the Wolf as the male seducer and the girl as on the verge of puberty. She's tempted by the Wolf's suggestions—to gather flowers, to listen to birdsong, to stray from the path—the very things her mother forbade her. It's an invitation to pleasure where pleasure 'morally' signifies as danger. Her red cloak, the colour of passion, of menstrual blood, advertises her as a sexual being but she is too young to comprehend what that may entail. It leads Red Riding Hood into a conversation with the Wolf, an 'unconscious' act, unconsciousness indicating, on her part, not only her unwillingness to analyse or understand her own behaviour but her inability to see where trouble lurks. In the bedroom scene, she doesn't 'recognise' the Wolf whom she has already met and so she is once again duped by him.

Bettelheim comments,

> if there was not something in us that likes the big bad wolf, he would have no power over us. Therefore, it is important to understand his nature, but even more important to learn

what makes him attractive to us. Appealing as naïveté is, it is dangerous to remain naïve all one's life.[16]

There are two dominant males in the story: the Wolf and the hunter. The Wolf is the representative of unbridled desire, he's treacherous and cunning. But finally he is the victim of his own appetites. He falls asleep after his feast, thereby leaving himself in jeopardy. The hunter is the good father, protective, astute and responsible, who saves Grandma and the girl. He is keen-eyed, necessary to his profession, which means he not only recognises the Wolf—'Do I find thee here, old sinner?'—but makes the inspired decision to cut open the Wolf, rather than shoot him. Red Riding Hood has learned her lesson from the combination of a good mother, whose advice she now values, and a good father who can defend and safeguard her. She emerges from the Wolf's belly reborn. 'How dark it was inside the wolf!' she remarks now that she is securely in the light—of awareness, of consciousness.

I saw the big bad Wolf while writing this chapter. I don't mean literally, of course, though it's extraordinary what may manifest when the current between the writer and her work flows intensely—inexplicable coincidences, sudden discoveries, images that arrive unannounced from the unconscious mind and slide into the real world like, well, magic.

I was walking towards a cafe and thinking about wolves when a man turned the corner with his leashed dog. It wasn't just any dog. It was a very large, very black, very shaggy German Shepherd with enormous paws. What startled me most was his height. If I were a little girl, he'd be nearly as tall as me. As it was his head was up to my waist. But this wolf was a kindly creature who flicked me a friendly glance from his amber eyes. His coat was glossy with health and care. He was obviously cherished. But if the dog bolted, his human would have been hard-pressed to restrain him, he was so mighty. After all, every domesticated dog on Earth is descended from the Wolf (*Canis lupus*). Somewhere in their psyches, do they remember wildness?

The tale continues to command interest. In her 2003 series on the subject, Portuguese–British artist Paula Rego presents the Wolf as an ageing, debauched-looking dancer. In *The Wolf Chats Up Red Riding Hood*, he's dressed to resemble a bizarre version of Grandma. But Red is not about to be easily seduced. Though the little girl sits near the Wolf, her arms are crossed in a gesture of resistance, and her expression is wary. She's small and thin and no match at all for the Wolf. It's a discomfiting scene which suggests predatory male sexual behaviour, paedophilia in fact. What is she learning from this man? What instruction is going on here? In the next scene, the Wolf lies asleep in bed as Mother plunges a pitchfork into his distended belly. Presumably he's eaten Red Riding Hood, as her cloak lies beneath him.

The final scene—*Mother Wears the Wolf's Pelt*—is ambiguous. Mother is the subject of the work. She sits cross-legged on a chair and has a confident, even a cheerful, expression. She's wearing a red hat and tight-fitting suit, an adult version of Red Riding Hood's garb, with the Wolf's pelt arranged around her neck. A stole, as it is known, was once a popular item of women's apparel. In the 1950s, when I was growing up, women wore fox stoles, a gruesome fashion item where the dead beast was made into a large fur collar. Its 'animality' was not expunged but emphasised: its eyes were shiny glass beads, its paws interlocked as a catch, its long furry tail hung down. I was fascinated by the sight of ordinary suburban women, whom I'd encounter on the tram or at church on Sundays, wearing slaughtered creatures around their shoulders.

Fur, of course, is not the prized fashion accessory it once was. In times past, fur connoted wealth, luxury and power; it was the privilege of the aristocracy and the upper classes. Following its popularity in the mid-twentieth century, in recent decades, vigorous (and sometimes violent) activism by PETA (People for the Ethical Treatment of Animals) and other animal rights groups has seen the fur trade substantially decrease in Europe. Major fashion designers like Michael Kors, Donatella Versace and Giorgio Armani have pledged not to use it, while American designer Tom Ford chooses *faux*.[17]

Mother touches the pelt with a sense of pleasure, even pride. She has defeated the Wolf but she has lost her daughter. It's a tragic victory but she doesn't emanate sadness, or even regret. She looks pleased with herself, robust and alert. Unlike the hunter, Mother was unable to save the child. She didn't pause to reflect: she went in for the kill.

Sarah Bonner considers that 'for Rego, the absence of the daughter means the mother's individual identity is asserted … In the final scene the mother is dressed in red with her own version of a red hood and the addition of the wolf skin muffler, reinforcing the message, contrary to psychoanalytical fairy tale interpretation, that age itself conveys knowledge, strength and cunning, ensuring the survival of the fittest.'[18]

Paula Rego, *The Wolf Chats Up Red Riding Hood*, 2003, pastel on paper, 84 × 67 cm, © Paula Rego, courtesy the artist and Victoria Miro.

Paula Rego, *Mother Wears the Wolf's Pelt*, 2003, pastel on paper, 84 × 67 cm, © Paula Rego, courtesy the artist and Victoria Miro.

Who knows? Did Mother want to get rid of her daughter all along? She assigned the child a perilous task. Was Mother jealous of the girl's budding sexuality, a competitor for male attention? In fairy tales, mothers (and stepmothers) often prove to be untrustworthy characters. Indeed, so concerned were the readers of the first volume of *Kinder und Hausmärchen*, with its bevy of treacherous mothers, that Jacob and Wilhelm, in subsequent editions, replaced them with 'stepmothers'.

Bettelheim's worthy successor is English author Angela Carter whose collection of short stories *The Bloody Chamber* (1979) confidently recast Little Red Riding Hood and other heroines for the contemporary feminist reader. Carter was well versed in fairy tales: she had completed a new translation of Charles Perrault, as well as imbibing Bettelheim. Provocative, erotic, brutal and witty, Carter's tales dispense with notions of innocence and safety, even of conventional reward.

In 'The Company of Wolves' she writes, 'You are always in danger in the forest, where no people are. Step between the portals of the great pines where the branches tangle about you, trapping the unwary traveller in nets as if the vegetation itself were in a plot with the wolves who live there.'[19]

The unnamed and dauntless heroine of the tale decides to traverse the winter woods to visit Grandma. It's Christmas Eve and she's menstruating. 'Her breasts have just begun to swell … and she has just started her women's bleeding, the clock inside that will strike, henceforward, once a month'. As she enters the forest, she hears 'the freezing howl of a distant wolf'.[20] She reaches for the carving knife she has placed in her basket. Suddenly a handsome young man, in hunter's kit and armed with a rifle, springs onto the path.

She's impressed. She's never seen such a fine fellow. He flirts with her and soon they're laughing and joking like old friends. He offers to carry her basket, and she acquiesces, 'unaware' she has sacrificed her weapon. Then the fellow suggests a wager. If he can reach Grandma's before her, by plunging off the path and trekking through the undergrowth, he'll win a bet. 'What would you like?'

the girl asks disingenuously. 'A kiss,' comes the reply.[21] After the hunter sets off, the girl dawdles. She wants him to arrive before her so he'll win the wager.

At Grandma's, the Wolf strips off his disguise, revealing his matted hair, hairy legs and genitals. 'Ah! Huge. The last thing the old lady saw in all this world was a young man, eyes like cinders, naked as a stone, approaching her bed.'[22] When the girl enters the house the Wolf reveals himself, and blocks her exit. But she's not afraid. Dialogue ensues but it takes a different direction. The girl asks the Wolf what she should do with her clothes. Throw them on the fire, dear one, the Wolf advises, you won't need them again. She does so. 'Now she was clothed only in her untouched integument of flesh. Thus dazzling, naked, she … went directly to the man with red eyes … and ripped off his shirt.'[23] When she comments on his big teeth—'All the better to eat you with'—the girl bursts out laughing. 'She knew she was nobody's meat.' And the happy ending? 'See! Sweet and sound she sleeps in granny's bed, between the paws of the tender wolf.'[24]

By exposing themselves to one another, 'freed' from their clothes, their socially acceptable or determined roles—the big bad Wolf, the naive girl—they can frankly appraise each other and create a surprising liaison. The girl, in her quest for knowledge, for sexual maturity, accepts that knowledge comes at a price— the death of her grandmother, the crone who bequeathed her the symbolic red cloak which must be dispensed with, burned. Instead of the girl being devoured, 'overwhelmed', by the Wolf's sensual appetites, she's a match for him. She laughs at his threatening words. She takes control of the situation by tearing off his shirt, triggering an erotic, transgressive encounter between animal and human, male and female, beast and babe. She seduces *him*, and by assigning the Wolf a submissive role, gives him the opportunity to be transformed into a gentle lover.

What of Jacob and Wilhelm? How fared the maestros of enchantment? What was *their* hero journey? The early years of their childhood were contented. In 1786, the brothers, their parents and siblings had a splendid abode in Steinau an der Strasse, near Kassel. Philipp, their father, was the district magistrate and the family lived in apartments adjoining the courthouse, a stately Renaissance structure built in 1562.

But the idyll ended in 1796 when Philipp suddenly died and the family lost their home and comfortable lifestyle. Though Jacob was eleven and his brother ten, they became the men of the family. The two struggled to attend school and then university, constantly reliant on family and friends. Circumstances worsened when their mother died, as well as their maternal grandfather who'd provided financial help.

During their education, the boys were keenly aware of their low social status. Poor boys didn't enter university in the late eighteenth century. The brothers rarely socialised with fellow students because it was too expensive. It made the Grimms studious, self-reliant and determined, and devoted to one another. In 1805, Jacob was forced to abandon his studies at Marburg University for a period to support the family, who were so impecunious that food was scarce.

The brothers were placed in the stressful situation of seeking wealthy benefactors to provide them with patronage and income. Thus their careers were enmeshed in delicate negotiations with illustrious aristocratic and intellectual individuals—including their law professor Frederick von Savigny and the writer Bettina von Arnim—to arrange their employment as librarians or academics. Their talent and commitment saw them succeed but it was an ongoing struggle.

In their early twenties, the young men began to collect folk tales.[25] While the emphasis was on Germanic stories, language and culture, some tales had been invented or collected by Perrault and the brothers modified them for a nineteenth-century German audience. There were local sources, too. Dortchen Wild, a family friend and neighbour, was an excellent raconteur. In 1825, she became Wilhem's wife. (Jacob did not marry but lived with Dortchen and Wilhelm).

Dorothea Viehmann was a peasant whom the brothers had met selling vegetables in a local market town. She was the most impressive storyteller they'd known. They wrote, 'She has retained these old stories firmly in her memory, a gift which she says is not granted to everyone. Indeed, many people can't even retain any tales, while she narrates in a manner that is thoughtful, steady and unusually lively. Moreover, she takes great pleasure in it.'[26]

A pivot of many fairy tales is a reversal of fortune. In *Cinderella*, for example, the girl's mother dies and so the child loses parental love and protection. Her father remarries—another bad stepmother!—and she is reduced to being a servant in her own home, sleeping in the ashes of the fireplace (hence her name) and harassed by her stepsisters. Of course, she is finally rescued by the prince.

Given the predicaments the brothers endured—the need to support younger siblings; being dogged by financial constraints and irregular earnings; becoming (unwittingly) involved in various political upheavals of their time; being overlooked for appointments that could have guaranteed them security—it's no wonder that the brave and lonely child, emblematic of fairy tales, must have resonated with Jacob and Wilhelm. How well they knew the journey of experience, encountered by the child in the forest (challenging circumstances) and the return home (safety, a successful outcome) because it was their own, repeated not once but many times.

The tales must have comforted them as, over the years, the brothers refined and republished them, attracting a growing audience as well as earning esteem for their assiduous research. The Grimms transformed themselves, as Jack Zipes notes, 'from a status as genial amateur antiquarians to eminent professors of philology'.[27]

In Germany today, fairytales are big business. The fairy-tale route is part of a 600-kilometre journey which stretches from the town of Hanau in central Germany (where the brothers were born) to Bremen by the North Sea (a reference to the tale *The Bremen Town Musicians*). The route tracks the Grimms, including places where they lived and worked as well as those linked to some of the stories. Several suitably picturesque towns have conjured a connection with the tales to earn the lucrative tourist dollar. In Alsfeld, for example, there's the House of Little Red Riding Hood, while Bad Wildungen offers a Snow White Museum, complete with performances by the Seven Dwarves, enacted by children.

There's also Hainich National Park, which is a protected primeval woodland in central Germany, a 'fairytale forest'. How I long for it! When planning this chapter, I also planned to travel to Germany and trek there, saturating myself with the rich, clean scents of its ancient Beech trees, stroking their mossy trunks and listening to the deep silence of the forest. But COVID-19 had other plans. So here I sit in July 2020, gazing at images on the internet, like much of the rest of the planet, frustrated and housebound.

While commercially driven and at times kitsch, the tourist treatment of the tales attests not only to their continuing popularity, fecund with imaginative possibilities that sees them renovated and restored for each new generation, but also to a path back to the awe, fun and magic of childhood.

Today the Grimms's lost childhood home in Steinau an der Strasse has become a museum celebrating their legacy. It's been restored to them—their memory at least. Such poetic justice is rare. I can't think of a happier ending.

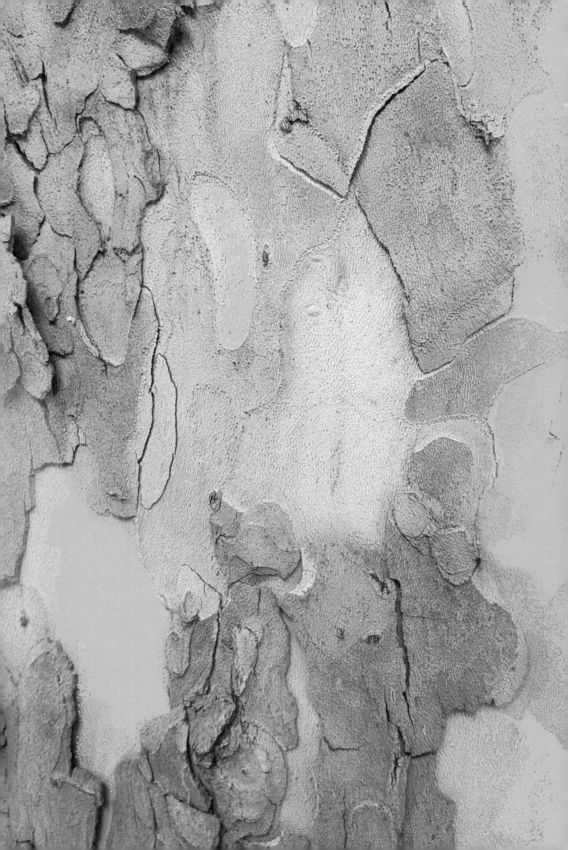

SENTIENCE

I INTERVIEWED AN AUGUST botanist for this book. I was interested in the scientific approach to trees and how it might
intersect with more lateral viewpoints, such as the possibility trees
are sentient. It's an issue I touched on when discussing Miranda
Gibson's tree-sit and something of which German forester Peter
Wohlleben, globally admired for *The Hidden Life of Trees*, has no
doubt. For me, the jury is still out. The pagan in me wants to
believe. The sceptic resists.

The Botanist and I met for coffee at Melbourne University
where I'm an honorary senior fellow. It's not as grand as it sounds.
The word honorary means I'm not paid a salary. Nonetheless, the
sinecure gives me access to the wealth of the university's libraries
and puts me easily in touch with some extraordinarily gifted and
generous academics.

The meeting didn't start promisingly. 'My wife said I should
be nice to you,' the Botanist announced. He was a short, barrel-
chested fellow with a flowing beard, around seventy. I don't mind
strong opinions so I wasn't discountenanced, though I could see,
from the start, pretty much where we were heading.

I've interviewed literally hundreds of people in the course
of my research, going back to the 1970s. So I have an array of
well-developed feints and manoeuvres to deal with even the
most intractable of subjects. Sometimes nothing works. I recall
interviewing Charles Blackman in one of Melbourne's stylish

Italian bistros. He'd been a close friend of Joy Hester's and I was writing her biography. Charles was so bored with my questions that he invited over a young guy at another table who'd approached Charles to gush his admiration. Charles then displayed an absorbed interest in all the young man said and completely ignored me.

I laughed. I was trying to disarm the Botanist. 'Oh dear,' I said, as if we were sharing a joke.

'Yes, I get very annoyed with these kinds of ideas. Plants do not have consciousness. They do not have a nervous system.' He was already quite riled. I thought of his wife thinking of us. Knowing how it would go.

'But Aboriginal people believe—'

'That is land management,' he said briskly.

It's more than that. It's faith, connection, the intersection between the natural and the supernatural. It's the matrix of the Dreaming. The landscape is full of stories, of signs. Country is an active, spiritual place.

I lowered my head and began to take notes. Playing for time. Acting respectfully while not feeling it. I'm reading the notes now, scattered across ten pages, in my little notebook. 'Nature doesn't have the capacity to self-regulate.' Then, surprisingly, 'Scientists are basically artists.' Er ... really? I mean, I'd never wish to deny a person's right to argue their work was artistic. Query, yes. Deny, no.

My own interpretation of art has broadened over the decades. In 2012, I wrote a book exploring the aesthetic qualities of birds' nests. I followed it up the next year by curating an exhibition at McClelland Sculpture Park + Gallery, on Victoria's Mornington Peninsula. For the show, also titled *Nest: The art of birds*, I selected nests from Museum Victoria's collection. I also included some lovely examples from the private collection of restaurateur Gay Bilson.

Planning the exhibition, my intent was to display the nests as small, exquisite sculptures, presenting them with the same cool, rigorous approach that governs human artworks. Some—of harmonious scale and materials—were grouped together, while most were displayed separately as unique objects to showcase their beauty, ingenuity and formal excellence.

Nest: The art of birds, 2013, installation view, Mark Ashkanasy, courtesy McClelland Sculpture Park+Gallery.

Displayed on white plinths and protected by perspex lids, the nests were focally lit in the long, white-walled gallery. I minimised natural light by sealing off a floor-length window on the gallery's rear wall so the viewer's gaze would be on the nests to the exclusion of all else. I wasn't surprised by how splendid the exhibition looked. I had every faith in the birds' abilities. In fact, at the opening, I thanked the birds for their contribution.

I didn't share these reflections with the Botanist. He already regarded me as a nitwit. Transgressing the sacred scientific attitude of objectivity, I was guilty of anthropomorphism. (Which, to me, translates as a lack of imagination.) I don't remember how the interview ended: I think we each wanted to get away from the other, our opinions intact.

The Gaia hypothesis, formulated by scientist James Lovelock in the 1970s, remains the most contentious in debates about sentience. It's what the Botanist meant when he said nature doesn't have the capacity to self-regulate. That's the pith of Gaia theory. It's gained a reputation as being somewhat 'New Age', as superficial popular science. But Tim Flannery believes 'it is anything but, being soundly based and profoundly important to our understanding of the evolution of life on Earth'.[1] Flannery notes that in universities it's often studied as Earth Systems Science, perhaps because that sounds more respectable. More recently, Lovelock described Gaia as

> A view of the Earth ... as a self-regulating system made up from the totality of organisms, the surface rocks, the ocean and the atmosphere tightly coupled as an evolving system ... this system [has] a goal—the regulation of surface conditions so as always to be as favourable as possible for contemporary life.[2]

So how does it work? For example, the Amazon rainforest can generate its own rainfall. There's an accumulation of moisture in the atmosphere over the Amazon that doesn't come from the seasonal rains, but scientists were never sure why. Recently, satellite data has shown that the increase coincided with a 'greening' of the rainforest, or greater proliferation of fresh leaves. It's water vapour released during photosynthesis, a process called transpiration, where plants create a liquid mist from small pores on the underside of their leaves. Thus the Amazon can regulate its own climate—as long as the destruction wrought by land clearing doesn't disrupt it.[3]

Of course, one reason Lovelock's theory earned him opprobrium from sections of the scientific community was due to its name—Gaia. Lovelock's neighbour William Golding, best known for his novel *Lord of the Flies* (1954) had suggested it. But in the hippie 1970s, for a scientist to name a hypothesis after a Greek goddess, Mother Earth herself, was outré. It even gave a spiritual slant to Lovelock's ideas and, as I'm sure the Botanist would concur, we can't have that.

Flannery believes that Lovelock's hypothesis is at least as contro-versial today as Darwin's theory of evolution was 150 years ago. But the fact an eminent scientist such as Flannery is respectful of the Gaia hypothesis indicates that Earth Systems Science is beginning to gain wider credibility.

Ecologist Monica Gagliano knows how dismissive scientists can be of those who push certain boundaries. She had been a marine ecologist and completed her PhD on coral reef fish. She'd relocated from Italy to James Cook University in Townsville to embark on the research, conducted on the Great Barrier Reef. At the end of Gagliano's experiment, when she had to kill the fish, the distress she experienced made her seek another scientific path. That's when she began studying plants.

When Gagliano announced to a university colleague that she was applying for a grant to research sound communication between plants, she was told it was career suicide. After reading her proposal at a grants workshop, another colleague sneered, 'Is this a joke? That is not science!' Gagliano knew he was not alone in feeling that way. 'In fact, many felt the same, but they preferred to stay silent, maintaining the appearance of decorous collegial behaviour, without realising their silence spoke volumes.'[4] Six months later, to Gagliano's surprise, she was awarded a three-year Australian Research Council fellowship. Having tried (and failed) to receive one of these lucrative, highly competitive and sought-after grants, I'd compare the process to running a marathon which lasts for weeks on end or learning a new language—fast. As far as academia goes, ARC grants are status-saturated, gold stars.

Gagliano's research *is* astonishing. She believes she can com-municate with plants and that they not only return the favour but initiate the contact. Plants are her guides and her inspiration. In 2015, Gagliano travelled to the Amazon lowlands of Peru where she sought advice and instruction from a shaman of the Shipibo people. A tree had 'called' her there.

In Australia, Gagliano had dreamed of the exact place where she would stay—a small stilt hut, its walls painted pastel blue and decorated with intricate geometric patterns. In the dream, Gagliano entered the hut to find an older man sitting by a fire. 'He was grinning at me with a flicker of satisfaction in his dark, narrow eyes as I sang a bizarre song made of sounds I could not hear and meanings I could not speak.'[5] She woke up that morning 'knowing that somewhere that hut, that man, and those strange songs were waiting for me'.[6] She searched Google and, eerily, 'amid the varied images I found the image of the hut, the person and a sketch of the direction to locate it'.[7] A few months later, she set off for the city of Pucallpa on the Ucayali River, a major tributary of the Amazon River.

There she met Don M who conducts healing ceremonies and curative rituals as the *curandero vegetalista* (plant shaman) for the local community. He was the same man Gagliano had seen in her dream. Don M told her that he'd been 'called' by the Socoba, a tropical tree also known as Bellaco-Caspi (*Himatanthus sucuuba*), which is rather like a Frangipani. The tree, designated as feminine by Don M, conveyed to him that she had appeared to Gagliano in the latter's dreams in order to summon her to Pucallpa. There Gagliano would undergo a ritual known as a *dieta* where she imbibed a hallucinogenic drink, made from the Socoba's bark, and receive instructive dreams and visions. The *dieta* was supervised by Don M. No money changed hands. The main message Gagliano learned—'the teaching that, in actuality, mattered the most'—was that not only could plants mysteriously yet clearly communicate with her but 'the plant is a teacher that will stay with you forever and keep teaching you in her own plant time'.[8]

Dietas contribute to South America's tourist dollar. Gagliano is but one of many First Worlders who have gone into the rainforest to seek healing from a shaman. On the web, you'll find plenty of lodges or retreats where the rituals are conducted. Take your pick. Choose your level of comfort, and find its price. Would you like a massage? Maybe a yoga class? Transfers from the airport? Hire a car? Then you can post your photographs and recommendations on Tripadvisor. It's known as ayahuasca tourism.

Ayahuasca (pronounced eye-ah-*wah*-ska) is the hallucinogen's most common name in South America.

While I commend Gagliano's courage and probity, I was startled to read online how readily the drug could be accessed. There seem no restrictions as to where, when, how often and with whom it's consumed. What about vulnerable people with mental health problems? Or those who might, throwing caution to the winds, mix the hallucinogen with alcohol or marijuana—a very bad idea, according to Australia's Alcohol and Drug Foundation.[9] Hopefully you'd be in the jungle with an experienced shaman who had successfully conducted the ritual many times and who could assist if you, literally, started to freak out. The shamanic interpretation of common and unpleasant side effects such as vomiting, nausea, screaming and weeping indicates the *dieta* is working.[10] The body's purge releases the mind from its constrictions.

Gagliano is disarmingly frank about the weirdness of her experiences. 'Rest assured,' she writes, 'that I did doubt my own sanity many times, especially when all of these odd occurrences started.'[11] Watching Gagliano talk about her research on YouTube, she seems funny, lighthearted, endearing, with a sharp mind and an ability to succinctly present complex issues.[12]

In a sense, Gagliano is merely modernising an ancient tradition. The Socoba, and other plants in the Amazon, have been used for their medicinal properties for centuries. The shamans are trained by older shamans who teach the younger ones (both women and men) the healing powers of the natural world. While Gagliano casts her adventure with the Socoba as one of spiritual enlightenment, the plant's bark has many useful and more mundane benefits.

For example, the Shipibo prepare a decoction of the bark to treat rheumatism. They also glean a milky white latex from the tree, either by breaking stems from the branches or 'wounding' the bark. Leslie Taylor writes that

Bellaco-Caspi is also popular as a natural remedy in Peruvian herbal medicine systems. It is considered a pain-reliever, blood cleanser, fever-reducer, astringent, anti-inflammatory and laxative. It is often employed for arthritis, rheumatism and back pain; cancer and tumours … [The latex is good for skin issues] such as wounds, abscesses, ulcers, boils, rashes and sores … [Bark and latex are also used for] gastric ulcers, intestinal and skin parasites (worms); and for tuberculosis and fevers. [13]

Taylor is the creator of the website *Rain-Tree Publishers*. She's a naturopath who worked with shamans and other Indigenous people in the Amazon, before founding a company that imported rainforest herbs and plants into the United States. Until 2012, that is, when the US Food and Drug Administration shut her down. Taylor's products had not been tested to FDA standards. Taylor's entry on Bellaco-Caspi is meticulous. She cites her own research and provides a regularly updated, comprehensive list of scholarly, scientific articles from peer-reviewed journals. If you wish to learn more about the Socoba's properties, it's a good place to begin.

We've wandered far from Elwood. But, while writing this chapter, a memory arose about an experience I had with a local tree and it's drawn me back. It's the Sugar Gum I mentioned on page 119, the tree where the Sulphur-Crested Cockatoos nest. It's a short stroll from my home in St Kilda Street. We share the same address, the tree and I. Writing about Gagliano awoke this memory because I've tussled with it just as I tussle with some of her conclusions. I think I buried the memory because it was too strange to confront.

One day, several years ago, as I was taking a walk that led me past the tree, I had a flash, a momentary vision. I 'saw' as the tree did. It was as though I was inside the tree, looking out. Or at least that's what it seemed. We humans are like flickers to the Sugar Gum,

Sugar Gum, Elsternwick Park Nature Reserve, Janine Burke, 2020.

who is deep in tree time. We appear and disappear from view very fast. It's like watching a speeded-up film or blips on the radar. Perhaps it's the 'slow time' Janet Laurence refers to in *Forest: Theatre of Trees* because it's time experienced differently. As Peter Wohlleben comments, trees *are* 'incredibly slow'.[14] Their childhood and youth last ten times as long as ours, while their complete lifespan is at least five times ours.

I'm shy about presenting this to you, dear reader, in case you think me an oddball. Even years later, I can't make head nor tail of it. I wasn't searching for the experience to validate my tree-loving credentials. It was long before I thought of writing this book. It arrived unannounced.

Charles Darwin, the father of modern biology, is best known for *On the Origins of Species* (1859), but he also wrote several volumes on plants. In 1880, he published *The Power of Movement in Plants*. He'd already published on climbing plants and insectivorous plants, which had stimulated his interest.

In this publication Darwin draws attention to the similarities between animals and plants in, for example, sensitivity to touch, light sensitivity and gravity. Darwin used various methods of inquiry: usually setting up exacting and controlled experiments which are clearly explained in the text, reporting the results and then drawing general conclusions. It not only interrupted the plants' rest, but Darwin's too.

> I think we have *proved* that the sleep of plants is to lessen the injury to the leaves from radiation. This has interested me much, and has cost us great labour, as it has been a problem since the time of [eighteenth-century Swedish naturalist Carl] Linnaeus. But we have killed or badly injured a multitude of plants.[15]

I admire Darwin for many reasons, one of which is for being the first authoritative voice to suggest that some birds have an aesthetic sense, in particular the male Bowerbird. In *The Descent of Man* (1871) he describes the Satin Bowerbird as offering 'the best evidence … of a taste for the beautiful'. In order to attract a female, the Satin Bowerbird collects 'gaily-coloured articles, such as the blue tail-feathers of parakeets, bleached bones and shells … These objects are continually re-arranged, and carried about by the birds while at play.'

Quoting bird-obsessive John Gould, Darwin writes that the Bowerbird's assemblages must be regarded as 'the most wonderful instances of bird-architecture yet discovered'.[16] In the days before time-lapse photography, Darwin, together with his son Francis, also a botanist, conducted experiments that involved staring—often for hours on end—at the plants. I like the humble patience of his approach, as well as the vivid way he described his discoveries.

What if I took a leaf out of Darwin's book? What if I visited the Sugar Gum daily for a week and sat there staring? What would I learn?

I'm not entirely ignorant of scientific methodology. I undertook an extensive reworking of Museum Victoria's rudimentary nest catalogue as part of the selection process for the exhibition at McClelland Gallery. It was slow and repetitious work but thrilling to actually hold the nests in my hands. With Jessie Smith, my astute research assistant, I measured, weighed and photographed the nests as well as identified the birds' building materials, the nest shape and other salient information. We called it a birdalogue.

I also noted the gender of the nest maker—or makers as the case may be—something I've not seen presented before. You can't escape gender, even in the bird world! Mostly, the nests are made by females. But there are couple endeavours. Mr and Mrs Magpie Lark combine to produce a nest—which is nigh on a perfect circle; I know, I measured it—and that's illustrated in this book. You can also read my catalogue entry in this endnote if you'd like.[17]

So here goes.

Magpie Lark Nest (foreground), Chough Nest (rear), Janine Burke, 2013. Collection Museum Victoria.

Day 1. Monday 27 July 2020. 12 p.m. It's a cold, windy day with light rain. I sit on a bench near the north-facing side of the trunk. How gorgeous it is! The bark is silvery white with passages of grey and beige that flow down the trunk as if painted by the assured hand of an abstract artist. Nature develops admirable and subtle colour compositions. I guess if you've got millennia to sort these things out, you'll either succeed (and evolve) or fail (and die out). I'm here for about ten minutes, getting colder and colder. A Currawong perches on a branch far above my head in the overstory, which is tossed by the wind.

Day 2. Tuesday 28 July 2020. 12 p.m. Chilly but sunny. A Magpie is carolling from the topmost branches. I sit in the same place, this time observing the gashes and fissures in the trunk. They're like wounds. A large one, stretching from the ground up about 1 metre, is raw and dark like the vagina of an Earth goddess, a portal to a subterranean world. I learn about the tree's ecosystem. On the trunk there are flying ants playing with the wind. In the fissures, I see several fresh webs made of glistening spider silk. The latter is useful for birds to help bind their nests together. I spot a wee spider abseiling down her web, probably checking if she's caught prey. I feel a little more still, a little less self-conscious.

Day 3. Wednesday 29 July 2020. 12 p.m. The sun has come out and the breeze has dropped, making for a mild winter's afternoon. I lie flat on my back on the bench, by far the best way to view the branches without craning my neck. Two Cockatoos arrive with a screech and settle themselves on a nearby branch. One has a wonky left eye. It seems damaged and is perhaps blind. One-eye it is. They cosy up and begin a meticulous grooming procedure, removing dirt and other irritants from each other's feathers. Clambering all over one another to make sure the job is done properly, they're a couple displaying affection and intimacy. In fact, the whole operation becomes more intimate when the male—One-eye—mounts the female. The grooming was foreplay and now they're having sex. One-eye seems quite the practised lover and the female is enjoying herself as she arches her neck for the bird equivalent of a kiss. Cute! I'll name her Cutie. So engrossed in lovemaking, One-eye and Cutie topple off the branch and fall into the air, screeching with surprise.

Day 4. Thursday 30 July 2020. 12 p.m. A surprisingly warm day for mid-winter. It's good to be outside. I take several close-ups of the tree. I'm sending them to Meyer Eidelson, the author of the informative booklet *Yalukit Willam: The river people of Port Phillip* (2014), who is steeped in all things Elwood. I'm also contacting St Kilda's EcoCentre. I need confirmation this is definitely a Sugar Gum. With 934 native species, identifying Eucalypts correctly can be time-consuming and complex, particularly for people unfamiliar with their different botanical characteristics (like me!). It's too early for blossoms (a prime species indicator), so I photograph the bark and a leaf. The branches are too high to reach, so I take a discarded leaf from the ground. It has a sinuous, oval shape and is about the length of my hand. It's pale green, mottled with small brown markings, with a sheen derived from the tree's rich oil. In Australia, the oil is prized for a myriad of health benefits including the treatment of coughs and colds (via inhalation), insect bites (via tincture) and a soothing rub for sore muscles.

Day 5. Friday 31 July 2020. 12 p.m. Another gloriously sunny day. I've started to look forward to my tree sessions. I return home feeling calmer, 'grounded'. I'm not a very calm person. My imagination is always busy and I need to give it lots of toys to play with. This book is a big toy. Observing the Sugar Gum's bark, I scrape off a piece and find beneath it an outraged spider whose home I've just invaded. Whoops. Then I remove from a fissure a small hunk of blood red, crystallised gum. (That's why Eucalypts are called Gums.) It's kino, an Indian name for the thick juice that exudes from a tree wound. It's been used extensively in tanning in India. At home, I pop the kino in a glass of water. It rapidly colours the water, first amber, then a rich, strawberry red. It's pretty and glowing as though I have a glass of fabulous liqueur on the kitchen bench. Kino does have health benefits—it's an astringent—but I won't be sipping it. I bet Darwin would.

Day 6. Saturday 1 August 2020. 12 p.m. It *is* a Sugar Gum. Identifying the tree was a five-person job. Meyer Eidelson wasn't sure, so he contacted Ben, his son-in-law, who's a horticulturist. Ben sent some images of gumnuts from a Sugar Gum and a River Red Gum to compare, but the gumnuts are too high for me to see. Then Neil and Zaylee from the EcoCentre get in touch and, yes, a Sugar Gum it is. I thank everybody on the Sugar Gum team. Then I post the information on the website of the Elsternwick Park Association, of which I'm a member. We're passionate about our park. Today a north wind is blowing and I'm careful about where I position myself because Eucalypts are notorious for dropping their branches when it's windy. I observe that inside the Sugar Gum is another tree, a dead tree. Some of its remaining thick, grey arms protrude from gaps in the living tree. The Cockatoos' nest is part of the dead tree so it continues to make a contribution to the ecosystem. Which, of course, is how nature works. When I get home, there's a pleasant surprise. The overstory of the Eucalypt that I can see from the kitchen window is 'my' Sugar Gum.

Day 7. Sunday 2 August 2020. 12 p.m. It's the last day of my experiment and it's also National Tree Day. Only discovered that this morning. Swear. The weather remains fine. The park is thronging with people. All the adults are wearing masks. In Victoria, we are encountering a huge spike in the numbers of infected coronavirus cases, meaning that even more stringent restrictions are ahead. It's been a demoralising week. I'm glad to be writing about trees, even happier to be sitting right in front of one. Facing the prospect of an English defeat during World War II, Virginia Woolf took refuge in nature. 'I worshipped the beauty of the country,' she mused. 'How [it] consoles and warms one.'[18] Indeed, Virginia. I lie on my back on the bench and listen to the tree. It's another north wind day. The sound the tree makes is soft and sibilant, shush … shush. I open my eyes and gaze upwards. The branches and leaves, caught by the wind's cross-currents, toss about like so many strands of glistening green hair. I think of all the tree offers us, all that we take from it, even this precious experience of beauty in the midst of adversity. What can I say but thank you. Happy National Tree Day, dear Sugar Gum. I feel better in your presence.

Thus my experiment comes to an end. I didn't encounter the earlier 'vision'. The tree didn't 'speak' to me. I didn't dream about it. However, I noticed a shift in mood, my spirits levelled and quietened. Of course, that's what we expect from nature. But does it have any scientific or biological basis? Or as immunologist

Qing Li asks, 'What exactly is this feeling that is so hard to put into words? ... What is this secret power of trees?'[19]

Based at Tokyo's Nippon Medical School, Qing Li is the author of several books on forest medicine. He declares himself a scientist not a poet. I guess he's trying to ward off the criticism levelled at Lovelock and Gagliano. *'I'm not crazy! I'm a bona fide scholar!'*

Qing Li's research draws on the Japanese practice of *shinrin-yoku* or forest bathing. Part of Japanese culture since 1982, *shinrin-yoku* offers stressed city dwellers a way to reconnect with nature, from walking in the woods, to strolling in the local park, to walking barefoot on your lawn. Qing Li's theory advances the notion that spending time around trees (even filling your home with plants and vaporising essential tree oils) can reduce blood pressure and lower stress as well as boost energy and the immune system.

The research Qing Li presents has been simplified to make it digestible for the non-specialist. But if you prefer his clinical trials and applications, they're available online. Qing Li spends the first section of *Into the Forest: How trees can help you find health and happiness* discussing his research and its results. Then, suddenly, in the chapter 'How To Practice Shinrin-yoku', it's as though a sedate and sensible person has burst into song. Qing Li declares,

> The forest is like our mother, a sacred place, a gift to us humans. It is a paradise of healing. Mother Nature fills us with wonder and curiosity and invites us in ... The art of forest-bathing is the art of reconnecting with nature through our senses. All we have to do is accept the invitation. Mother Nature does the rest.[20]

Qing Li comments on Mary O'Brien, professor of oncology at The Royal Marsden Hospital in London. In 2004, she was the first person to prescribe *Mycobacterium vaccae* for humans. It's a harmless microbe found in compost and healthy soil that can stimulate the production of mood-lifting neurotransmitters. Trialling it with her lung cancer patients in the hope of boosting their immune systems, O'Brien discovered that her patients were noticeably happier after taking the serum. In fact, they claimed to be experiencing less pain than their control group counterparts.[21] So, combining the microbe with chemotherapy does offer tangible benefits. It may not cure the patient, or even prolong their life, but feeling upbeat is surely a godsend during a serious illness.

O'Brien's research also underscores the relationship between our immune system and our emotions. When we walk in the forest, we breathe in *Mycobacterium vaccae* and it enhances our mood. Every gardener knows the pleasure of digging in the earth with their hands. Now science can go some way towards explaining why. And so this chapter comes to an end. Time for some *shinrin-yoku*!

TREES AS WITNESSES

IT WAS THE one cold day I experienced in Louisiana. The wind was chilly, bitter, insistent as it wrapped around my legs and tugged at my jacket. My hands had turned a fine, mottled blue. In New Orleans, even if the morning was mild, the steamy heat rose by midday, and I was used to dressing lightly in a cotton blouse and leggings.

It was 2015 and I was at Evergreen Plantation, about an hour's drive north from the city along River Road and halfway to Baton Rouge. There's a lot of sky to see in the lush, flat, green Louisiana landscape. Today it hung low, grey and cloud-laden. Occasionally a drop of rain touched my cheek as if the sky could not quite make up its mind to rain or not. I was feeling slightly numb. It wasn't only the weather.

The day before, Good Friday, I'd been rushed to the emergency ward at the Tulane University Hospital for a pain that gripped my guts like a fist. It was as though something inside me was awake and angry. But as I lay on the hospital trolley, the spasms gradually eased, and I refused the morphine the nurse offered. The CAT scan, the x-rays, the blood test all returned clear. They couldn't find anything wrong with me. I'd been shivering on the trolley. I was shivering still.

Evergreen was one of the main reasons I'd come to Louisiana. I was researching my great-grandfather Lawrence Burke. I didn't know him—he died in 1912. But I knew his face. His photograph hung in the dining room in the long, dark, damp, leaking house in Malvern that my parents rented from my great-aunt Norah. His expression was stern, the eyes unrelenting in their fixedness. That's all I can remember—not his features, just his eyes. He frightened five-year-old me.

It was Norah who told my parents that her father had been a slavedriver in the South. 'He drove slaves across America,' my mother recalls Norah telling them proudly. More recently, my mother followed it up with Nance, my uncle Leo's former wife, who lives in Queensland. Yes, Nance knew the story, too. When we first heard it, none of us was shocked or disgusted. No-one felt guilty or complicit. America and the slave trade were worlds away from white, middle-class, 1950s Australia. The notion of African slavery was more than exotic: it was incomprehensible.

On its website, Evergreen boasts it's the most intact plantation in the South, with thirty-seven of its buildings on the National Register of Historic Places. Most were built prior to the Civil War (1861–65). Evergreen was and remains a working sugar plantation. It covers more than 900 hectares that includes a swamp and a section of Lac des Allemands.

The Big House, the residence of the plantation owner and his family, was originally built in 1790 and was renovated in 1832. It's splendid and imposing in the Greek Revival style with Doric columns, wide balconies and a romantic, sweeping, double staircase. Fanlights grace the main doors and green French shutters flank the floor-length windows. Painted brilliant white and set amid lawns and manicured gardens, Evergreen is the picture perfect image of a Southern mansion. It's *Gone with the Wind*.

Evergreen has appeared in film. Quentin Tarantino shot part of his angry, confronting movie *Django Unchained* (2012) there.

Evergreen Plantation, Louisiana, Janine Burke, 2015.

Jamie Foxx played the lead, a freed slave searching for his wife. The couple had been separated when they were sold. In the scenes shot at Evergreen, Django exacts bloody vengeance on the white slave-drivers who work at the plantation—an episode which sees him (literally) get away with murder. The climax of the movie takes Django to Candieland, the home of Calvin Candie (Leonardo DiCaprio), its sadistic boss. The denouement is a bloodbath when Django, to rescue his wife Broomhilda (Kerry Washington), murders Candie, as well as sundry others, then blows the house to kingdom come.

At Evergreen, each building however humble was designed for aesthetic effect. The two garçonnières at the rear of the house are elegant brick bungalows where the lads of the family and visiting males were billeted. The matching, freestanding towers known as pigeonniers, where pigeons and squab were bred for the table, were, our tour guide Deeann tells us, something of a status symbol in their day. Even the Greek Revival privy which faces the parterre garden shows an eye for detail, decoration and flamboyance. Richard Sexton describes it as 'a diminutive temple monument to nineteenth century human hygiene'.[1]

The effect of Evergreen and its surrounds, underscored by the doubling of staircase, garçonnière and pigeonnier, is of an exact and lovely symmetry, a precise arrangement determined by people of wealth, taste and style.

Deeann is brisk, smart, informative. She's a graduate history student at Louisiana University. Her choice of a summery pink blouse on this cold day seems a bit optimistic. We rib her about it but she just smiles. On the tour this morning, there are probably twenty of us, of a variety of generations.

Deeann shows us into the house. There's antique furniture, a four-poster bed covered with a glossy quilt, portraits, china, embroidery, rugs. The interior is so meticulously curated and evocative it's as though Evergreen's former inhabitants had, moments before, glided away. Deeann charts the dynasty of French Creole families who bought the land in the eighteenth century and who hung on to it until the 1930s when a series of disasters struck, including a record-breaking flood, a blight on the cane and, last but not least, the Great Depression. The property was going to ruin when it was bought in 1946 by oil heiress and philanthropist Matilda Geddings Gray who began the massive task of restoring it and who, in 1998, opened it to the public.

Deeann leads us outside. The tour is nearly finished but there's one more place to visit. We traverse a long avenue of Southern Live Oaks (*Quercus virginiana*), their branches festooned with drifts of Spanish moss whose tendrils float in the breeze like tresses of mist. The property takes its name from them. The Oaks are around three hundred years old with magnificent, gnarled, lichen-dappled trunks. Overhead their branches touch, forming a luminous green canopy. Sequestered from River Road and the Big House, it's as if we've entered an enchanted realm.

Then we see the cabins. Laid out in two neat rows, they are where the enslaved lived prior to the Civil War. It's the reason Evergreen is unique. There's nowhere else in the South where a slave village can be found. The simple, Cypress wood huts are not wholly original; they've been somewhat restored over the years as weather and wear took their toll. Emerald moss, the exhalation of Louisiana's humidity, clings to the walls. At the end of the avenue stretch the cane fields where the slaves were forced to work. Hard. During the frantic season when the sugar was harvested and manufactured, their days started before sunrise and ended after dark, seven days a week. Often the children, too. In a census prior to the Civil War, the official count of slaves at Evergreen was 103. By any estimate in the Deep South, Evergreen was a big business. Plantations of its size were factories and their purpose was to produce a cash crop on a massive scale for a global market.

Slave Cabins, Evergreen Plantation, Louisiana, Janine Burke, 2015.

The group has gone quiet. Deeann is talking but I can't concentrate on what she says. I'm in the state of shock you encounter in a collision. A moment felt so intently you can't quite grasp it. When reality becomes too real. It's the clash between two dissonant experiences. There's the aesthetic realm of the trees and the ugly truth of the cabins. Nature's languid, extravagant, captivating beauty set against the tangible proof of suffering and injustice. They exist together: profound beauty, profound cruelty. The little houses do not symbolise inhumanity: they embody it. A state-sanctioned system of violence can be touched. Here, as I stand on the stoop. It can be entered. Here, as I walk into a small room with rough-hewn furniture.

The cabins are made of Bald Cypress (*Taxodium distichum*), an incredibly tough tree that grows in water, in the endless swamps, creeks and rivers of Louisiana. They rise like giants from their liquid homes. They're not evergreens—that is, they are deciduous and lose their leaves unlike the Oaks—and it's why they've earned the name bald because that's the effect when the leaves die.

Evergreen's name draws attention not only to the importance of the Oaks but their symbolism as ever growing and ever renewing, a hideous connection given the place's history. It's the story of the South in a nutshell: slavery was endemic and exonerated at all levels of society. Some religious folk were against it, but most preached its benefits. It was the sad, sick stain of the South, meant to be 'evergreen' due to the ruthless subjugation of African-American people and their huge contribution to the economy. Some slaves were freed by their masters, some—daring and desperate—escaped to the north. Others became slavedrivers themselves with the power to torment their own people.

Harriet Beecher Stowe's *Uncle Tom's Cabin* (1852) is the immensely popular novel that helped to raise awareness about Southern slavery and set the stage for the Civil War. In the novel's finale, it's two African-American slavedrivers, Quimbo and Sambo, who, at the behest of Simon Legree, the loathsome plantation owner, beat Uncle Tom to death. *Uncle Tom's Cabin* might appear sentimental to contemporary taste but Beecher Stowe didn't ignore the fact that some African-American people were complicit in slavery's tyranny.

The slave quarters are perfectly laid out. There's an echoing symmetry: the doubling of cabins and trees with Evergreen's buildings and staircase. The front of the plantation is a like composed face, a cultivated manner, a refined bearing behind which is the brutal expression, the fierce cruelty, the truth of how that splendid way of life was generated and maintained.

A boy in our group asks Deeann what the people here ate.

'They gave them pork. They were Muslims. It was another insult.' It's an African-American man in his early thirties. He's handsome, powerful. He's shouting. 'Nothing good happened here. *Nothing*.' He marches away from us.

Deeann says quietly that the people who lived here were Christians. But I don't care. I'm grateful for the man's anger. What do I have the right to say? Was he here? Did Lawrence come to this place? Am I literally following in his footsteps? What the hell does that make me? An innocent bystander? Somehow involved? A ghoul?

Planning my journey from Melbourne, I'd no idea how I'd reach Evergreen. It's isolated and there's no public transport from New Orleans. Hire a car? I felt too timid to take the wheel. After all, Americans drive on the wrong side of the road. Perhaps I could pay someone to drive me and wait the two or so hours while I joined the guided tour—the only way to visit Evergreen. How much would that cost? Maybe my hotel staff would advise me.

Shortly after I arrived in New Orleans, I met Phyllis and Jim Wagner. Phyllis liked to say, 'We picked Janine up in the bar of the Hotel Provincial.' Frustrated at being unable to get internet in my room, I'd parked myself and my laptop in the hotel's bar, armed myself with a glass of wine, and began trying to open my email.

'How are you doing with that?' a woman inquired.

Even by my second evening in New Orleans, I was used to people, wherever I might be, striking up a conversation. It seemed a city full of strangers eager to connect. The woman wore round, gold-rimmed glasses and a little straw hat at a rakish angle. A grey plait curled around her shoulder. All her clothes were varying shades of bright pink, some solid colour, some patterned.

'Bloody slow.'

She laughed. 'Oh, that's New Orleans. It's notorious for bad internet. It's been like that for the last few days. That's why I'm here. I was trying at home and it didn't work.'

Later she rang my room. We'd not exchanged names but by dint of explaining to the hotel clerk that I was the Australian (a rare commodity in New Orleans), that I'd checked in only recently, and, due to what I came to admire as Phyllis's disarming combination of persistence and grace, she tracked me down.

'Come to our place and eat crawfish with us on our balcony. We're a block away. We're waiting for you.' The invitation, generous, polite, direct, brooked no opposition.

In the mild evening air, I made my way carefully down Chartres Street. With good reason. The French Quarter, the gorgeous eighteenth-century heart of New Orleans, is fissured with broken, slippery sidewalks and pot-holed roads. It's like finding a slice of the Third World in a neighbourhood of Paris. The Quarter is also party central. Loud guys with litre-deep daiquiris in plastic glasses staggered down Bourbon Street while holidaymakers wandered across the roads, apparently oblivious to the cavalcade of traffic and the mule-drawn sightseeing carriages. I'd observed more than one tourist hobbling on crutches or with an arm hoist in a sling and I didn't intend to join their ranks.

I passed the high white walls of the Old Ursulines Convent and next to it St Mary's Italian Church to spy Phyllis sitting in a pool of light on a first-floor balcony, waving to me. I was introduced to Jim, a white-haired, square-jawed and bespectacled fellow in his late sixties. Earthy and relaxed, he set me at ease with his quick sense of humour. Phyllis fussed about, pouring me a glass of wine and insisting I start on the bowl of crawfish, which resembled a collection of little rubbery lobsters. Their friend Anna was also there. In town for a conference, she worked in education at Denver Art Museum. She was a softly spoken, young, African-American woman with a long, smooth, beautiful face and a halo of wiry hair.

When Phyllis asked me why I was in New Orleans, I stared at Anna, confused, embarrassed. 'My great-grandfather was a slavedriver. I think he might have come here before he went to Australia.'

There was a pause. Then Anna said, 'No-one talks about that.' Evenly. Without accusation. Just interested. What did I expect her to do? Dump the crawfish bowl on my head?

Her statement spoke of several things. Firstly, I was naive, indeed ignorant, about how an African American would respond to my research. Secondly, I hadn't realised that telling the story of having a slavedriver in the family was uncommon. I knew that after the Civil War those who'd been in the trade disguised or buried their past, often describing themselves as property dealers. Which is what they were and how slaves were regarded. Items to be appraised and auctioned, bought and sold. It strikes me that some of those families remain in New Orleans, keeping quiet about the past, about *their* great-grandfathers.

'Why are you writing about it?' Anna asked. Again her tone was curious, gentle.

Because I'm a writer and I ask questions. Because it fascinates and horrifies me. Because what he did was wrong. 'I'm trying to make sense of it.'

'He was young?'

'Yes.' She shrugs. I realise I want Anna to castigate him. Enact rage. Instead there's a trace of sympathy in her tone.

A little later, Anna left. She had sessions to attend the following morning at the convention centre in the Warehouse District, New Orleans' arts precinct.

I settle into another glass of wine with the Wagners. Phyllis and Jim are retired New Yorkers. Like many, they'd felt the tug of New Orleans' idiosyncratic charm, its constant and determined festivity and its embracing sense of community, and decided to settle there. But not all of the year. To escape the summer's claustrophobic humidity and its threat of hurricanes, they decamped to their home in New York state, not far from Buffalo. It was where they'd met in the 1970s when Phyllis was studying to be a teacher and Jim a psychiatric social worker.

When I explained I wanted to visit Evergreen, Phyllis spontaneously offered to take me. Overwhelmed by such generosity, I stammered out protestations. 'But we've been wanting to get out there,' Phyllis insisted. 'You've given us the opportunity.'

The year before I'd tracked down records which had taken me to Kilkenny, Lawrence's birthplace in Ireland. Kilkenny is a pleasant, unremarkable town on the banks of the River Nore, adorned with a twelfth-century Norman castle, its chief tourist attraction. His parents were Thomas Burke, a farmer, and Judith Purcell. He had three brothers, Patrick, Michael and William, and an elder sister who was born in 1822.

Lawrence's obituary confirmed he'd spent time in America before heading to Australia. It didn't say where. Trying to find documentary evidence to confirm when Lawrence left Ireland and where he landed in America was like trying to find a needle in a haystack. A needle I have never found. Even his birth date was uncertain, ranging from 1827 (on his death certificate) to 1834 (on his marriage certificate). When I came across a Lawrence Burke who'd arrived in New Orleans, the location of the biggest slave auction in the South, in 1851, my curiosity was sufficiently piqued, and I decided to follow him there.

There's historical richness and tragedy in this brief account of his Irish years. In the autumn of 1845, blight had struck the potato crop across Ireland. In Kilkenny about one-third of the crop was affected. While there'd been many potato blights from the eighteenth through to the nineteenth century, this was a new type. *Phytophthora infestans* is an air-born fungus which transforms both planted and stored potatoes into inedible rot. For the rural poor it meant disaster. The population in Kilkenny was close to 200000 and poverty was already widespread. Illiteracy was high and many lived in appalling conditions.

Lawrence would have witnessed terrible sights—ill, malnourished, homeless people, clad in rags, barefoot even in winter. Big-eyed skeleton-children with ricketty joints. Death bloomed in Ireland. Had Thomas and Julia died, prompting Lawrence's departure? It was certainly a good time to leave. In 1851, the blight caused the famine known as the Great Hunger. From May to December that year, nearly five thousand people emigrated from County Kilkenny. Villages became ghost towns and *slàn* (goodbye) the melancholic refrain. Brutalised by his experiences, did it mean Lawrence could brutalise others?

The cheapest passage across the Atlantic was from Liverpool to New Orleans. The journey lasted around six weeks. Though Lawrence was crammed into steerage, it was a far more comfortable journey than that endured by African people. Until the slave trade was banned by the British, Liverpool had played a key role in its operation. Ships loaded with guns, ammunition and cotton sailed to ports in the Congo (which comprised areas of present-day Republic of Congo, Democratic Republic of Congo and Angola) where the goods were sold or exchanged for people kidnapped by African slavers, at the behest of a local king or wealthy merchant. Incarcerated in coastal forts, the Africans were shackled by the neck and ankle, then packed into ships and transported to New Orleans.

For Lawrence, arriving in New Orleans must have been a dazzling experience. Here was the New World where he would make his fortune. After Ireland's cold, wet misery, he would have been enveloped in Louisiana's sensual, humid warmth. New Orleans was a bustling, cosmopolitan port city, founded by the French, graced with stylish architecture, fine restaurants and shops

displaying luxury European goods. On the levee of the Mississippi
River, the fashionable crowd, some of whom were freed slaves,
promenaded. Among the French, German, Spanish and Creole
people who made up the population, the largest migrant group
was the Irish. Lawrence would have joined a boisterous and tight-
knit community. The roughest section of the city was the Irish
Quarter of St Thomas Street or, as novelist George Washington
Cable commented, 'the filthy Irish Quarter'.[2] For the newly arrived
slave, however, the experience was utterly painful, alienating and
bewildering. Some tried to escape, some committed suicide. Many
were flogged into submission.

Slavery was booming in the South, even though the importation
of slaves from Africa had been banned since 1808. Not only was
there smuggling along the coast, there was also a lucrative market
for owners who could sell 'chattels' from one state, one plantation,
one auction house, to another. Lawrence was literate and he could
ride. He'd learned on the lively, hardy horses of Kilkenny.

The driver, or overseer, was based on a plantation. His task was
to ensure a high crop yield and he always carried his whip when he
rode into the fields to goad and monitor the slaves. Mostly young,
poor and white, the drivers were a despised class. Feared by the
slaves, because they were often harsh, and disliked by plantation
owners because they could be disreputable and unruly, the drivers'
tenure on most plantations was short. Slave women were fair game
and Lawrence may have had sexual experiences with them.

But Lawrence 'drove slaves across America'. Which means as
well as being a driver, he was also a trader, a businessman. During
'the slave season', May to December, the traders bought slaves
from plantation owners, breaking up families and friendships, and
severing communal ties. The arrival of the trader was greeted with
dread by the slaves. It's the kind of situation that caused Django's
separation from his wife Broomhilda in Tarantino's film. On the
long walk south, male slaves were chained together in a 'coffle'
while the women, who were not chained, carried the younger
children and followed behind.

Lawrence could have then driven them from, say, Kentucky to New Orleans, a journey of around 1200 kilometres that could take up to eight weeks. A comparable journey would be from Coffs Harbour to Melbourne. The agricultural economy was undergoing massive change. The Old South states such as Virginia and Kentucky were dispensing with the labour-intensive crops of tobacco and cotton, and switching to grains. Plantation owners no longer needed large numbers of workers. The Deep South states, like Louisiana and Georgia, who were heavily investing in cotton as well as sugar cane, were desperate for cheap labour. It led to the second, massive, enforced migration of African people.

That's what happened to Uncle Tom. He lost the cosy family home he shared with Chloe, his wife, and their children on the Kentucky plantation where he lived and where he'd had kindly owners. By making it the title of her book, Beecher Stowe emphasised that painful wrench. From there Tom was taken to New Orleans. I'll let Beecher Stowe describe it. Her research is impeccable.

> The slave-dealer collects his gang in Virginia or Kentucky, and drives them to some convenient, healthy place,—often a watering place,—to be fattened. Here they are fed full daily; and, because some incline to pine, a fiddle is kept commonly going among them, and they are made to dance daily; and he who refuses to be merry—in whose soul thoughts of wife, or child, or home, are too strong for him to be gay—is marked as sullen and dangerous, and subjected to all the evils which the ill will of an utterly irresponsible and hardened man can inflict upon him. Briskness, alertness, and cheerfulness of appearance, especially before observers, are constantly enforced upon them, both by the hope of thereby getting a good master, and the fear of all that the driver may bring upon them if they prove unsalable.[3]

When Lawrence left the United States for Australia, his journey was financed by the slave trade.

By 1863, he had shares in a mine in gold-mad Ballarat. Rich, bold and raffish, it was a frontier town that was fast gentrifying itself into a modern city. It's the traditional home of the Wathaurong people, many of whom had been dispossessed of their lands due to the gold rush. In the streets of Ballarat, it must have been strange for Lawrence to see people who might have been both poor and black, but who had never been sold into slavery.

Though Lawrence bought shares in mines, those were investments: he wasn't going to get his hands dirty. His new career was inspired by his work in the South: he became a publican. Driving the slaves meant resting at hotels on the long trek to New Orleans. It was where the traders met up, swapped notes and drank whiskey. There they assembled the pens where the slaves were kept shackled at night, gave them food and drink, perhaps even some minimal medical care. The road was dangerous. Slaves conspired to escape, and often managed to do so. Then the trader would hire a patrol to hunt them down, or do so himself. He needed to be constantly alert, ready with the whip or the gun.

Perhaps Lawrence sought to recapture the male camaraderie of the pub, the boozy gossip of the bar, the welcome, home-cooked meal and the clean bed after days on the road. It was also a family concern: the men out the front, pouring the drinks and keeping order, the women in the kitchen or serving in the dining room. It was an example Lawrence successfully re-created in Victoria where he was the licensee of a number of hotels. In 1884, he built the Terminus Hotel in Wycheproof, in the state's north-west, which stands to this day. He also acquired several properties in the district, land that he left to his children. When I visited the hotel a few years ago, and introduced myself, the publican shouted me a drink.

In 1864, Lawrence had married Margaret Grace, a County Tipperary lass, who lived in Geelong. The couple had twelve children, eight of whom survived. Norah was the third child. Patrick, my grandfather, was the seventh. He, too, became a prosperous publican in rural Victoria. The family tradition continued. His son, my uncle Leo, managed the hotel bar while sisters Molly and Greta took care of the dining room and accommodation. The family are esteemed in Yarrawonga and the hotel (now under different management) is named Burkes Royal Mail.

Okay, so this journey didn't turn into an episode of *Who Do You Think You Are?* It's left me tantalised, bemused, intrigued and bloody frustrated. Perhaps all I can do is simply this—present what the trees of Evergreen showed me, and be myself a witness.

Last night in New Orleans. I'm in the bar of the Hotel Provincial, waiting for Phyllis and Jim to come by before we head out to dinner.

I ask James, the bartender, what makes a good publican? Did that mean an outgoing, buoyant personality? James is in command of his job, mindful, professional, friendly but not too much so.

'It depends,' he replies. 'If you're the only game in town, maybe not. But that's the joy of it. Making people happy. Looking after them.'

Looking after them. Kind of chilling given Lawrence's work in the South. But Lawrence knew how to take care of his family. Maybe after escaping the chaos the famine visited upon Ireland, after seeing African-American families broken apart and the victims hauled from one state to another, stability was key. This tough, astute man was adored by his family. The large gravestone that his family erected to him and wife Margaret in the Wycheproof cemetery seems proof of that. Lawrence's death certificate describes him as a farmer. He wasn't. He owned but didn't farm the land. But that's how Thomas, his father, described himself on his marriage certificate. It's a link that shows how far, literally and symbolically, Lawrence travelled. I suppose I shouldn't begrudge Lawrence the pride he felt in his achievements, regaling his family with tales of his amazing adventures.

But I remember his eyes, unnerving me.

Several years ago, I went to Nuremberg to research Albert Speer
and Leni Riefenstahl for an ongoing project on artistic partnerships from the late nineteenth to the late twentieth century. I chose
them to deliberately make the point that not all collaborations
are commendable.

In 1933, when Hitler grasped power as German Chancellor, he
commandeered Nuremberg Park as the Nazi Party Rally Grounds.
Each summer until 1938, hundreds of thousands of people flooded
into the medieval city and then travelled out to the rally grounds,
to attend the totalitarian spectacle of the Party Rally. A massive
building programme commenced when architect Albert Speer was
appointed by Hitler as the site's designer.

Speer shaped the Nazi aesthetic and his taste for a monumental
neoclassical style mirrored Hitler's. In post–World War I Vienna,
a period when Hitler strived and failed to become an artist, he
became obsessed with urban design. By collaborating with Speer,
Hitler realised his architectural ambitions. Describing himself as the
Supreme Master Builder of Germany, Hitler decided to position
Nuremberg as the historical centre of the 1000-year Reich.

The 1934 Nazi Party congress, staged by Speer, was an elaborate
event in Nuremberg. Speer designed the Zeppelin Field, a stadium
with standing room for 150 000 people. Speer also designed the
parade grounds, which included the Luitpold Arena and the Great
Road, which is 2 kilometres long and 60 metres wide. Architects
Ludwig and Franz Ruff designed the gigantic Congress Hall, based
on the Colosseum, meant to seat 60 000 party faithful. That year,
Hitler also commissioned actress and director Leni Riefenstahl to
film the propaganda documentary *Triumph of the Will*. Speer and
Riefenstahl became friends: Riefenstahl filmed the spectacle that
Speer created.

Draconian anti-Semitic legislation, known as the Nuremberg
Laws, was enacted at the Party Rally in 1935. It meant Jewish
people were segregated from society, lost their political rights and
were forbidden to marry those 'of German blood'. It paved the way
for the Holocaust. As Hitler prepared for war, construction on the

rally grounds ceased, leaving many sites unfinished. But quarries all over Germany continued to supply stone for the rally grounds. Concentration camps were established near several quarries where the prisoners were exploited for their labour.

Fittingly, in 1945, Nuremberg was chosen by the Allies to host the trials of Nazi leaders including Albert Speer, Hermann Göring and Rudolf Hess.

Increasing numbers of people wishing to learn about Nuremberg's role in the Third Reich led, in 2001, to the creation of the documentation centre, commissioned by the city of Nuremberg, and designed by Austrian architect Günther Domenig. It's visited by thousands of people each year. The centre documents the rise of Nazism, the Nuremberg rallies, the outbreak of war and the oppression and murder of millions of people. Throughout the grounds there are information plaques with historical data and images.

To reach the grounds, I caught a taxi from my hotel in central Nuremberg, a journey of around fifteen minutes. I think there was a tram but I had neither the time, nor the command of German, to find it. It sounded creepy when I gave the driver directions. Did he consider me a Holocaust tourist? Was I?

The documentation centre is the first, and often the only, stop for visitors to the grounds. The tour buses deposit visitors there and return a few hours later. Inside, there's a bookshop and a cafe. The centre teems with school groups, families and people on holiday but the crowds at the centre give lie to the experience of the site. Walking through the grounds, I did encounter other visitors, sometimes alone or in small groups. But there were few of us, despite the fine weather on the cusp of summer. Perhaps the response to the centre, of being on the site where Nazi spectacle and policy was enacted, a place which demonstrates some of the worst episodes of human history, and where its crimes are chronicled in minute detail, made further investigation of the grounds unbearable.

After I left the documentation centre, I lay on the bank of the lake. I was exhausted by waves of powerful emotions: disgust, anger, sadness, the desire to do something, the impossibility of doing anything. I registered the air was still and warm, even though the day was overcast. It felt good to be resting on the earth. The fine branches of Silver Birches provided shade. Bevies of Greylag Geese and their goslings swam past on the lake.

About an hour passed before I began to think coherently, and then more time before I decided to take photographs. Nothing big, I decided. Not at first. Nothing built by Nazis. Water. Reflections. Trees. Reeds. A duck's downy feather that decorated the grass like a jewel. A man and his granddaughter. The little girl, wearing a bright pink dress, wanted to play with the geese. She waved and called to them but they weren't interested and swam away from her. The man and I exchanged smiles.

I circuited the Congress Hall and reached the Great Road. It's unfinished and goes nowhere. It's now used as a car park. The Great Road is so vast that as I walked, I didn't seem to make any progress, as if space and time had collapsed. I felt the pressure of being alone in a place which was designed to be shared by thousands of the Nazi Party faithful. You weren't meant to be alone. Alone was wrong, illicit, the fate of the outsider, the victim. The victor is surrounded by comrades, marching forward in precise formation. Though the Great Road was empty and silent, it seemed crowded and noisy. Like the rest of the grounds, it was replete with voices, cries, memories, echoes of the dreadful ideas the place embodies.

I'm not brave. I could never visit Auschwitz, though my friends Suzanne Heywood and Isaac Schweitzer went there and said Kaddish, a mourning ritual that celebrates God despite loss and death. I don't have such courage. I'd be too afraid that my imagination would meet a reality that could destroy me, or that my dreams would be haunted forever. At fourteen, Anne Frank's diary was my 'negative epiphany', a term Susan Sontag used to describe her introduction to the Holocaust when she saw photographs of the camps.[4]

Hitler strived to create a phoney history for Germany at Nuremberg, a royal lineage that went back centuries, that would establish Nuremberg as the holy city of the Reich. Nuremberg had no such authenticity, but Hitler's genius for propaganda meant he attracted those—like Speer, Riefenstahl and Joseph Goebbels— who used the art forms of architecture and film to flesh the myth. Nuremberg was Rome and Nuremberg Park became the Nazi Party playground where, each summer, thousands camped, marched and hailed their Führer. Since assuming power in 1934, Hitler had, by 1939, a generation of young men, trained like warriors in the Hitler Youth movement, who were prepared to go to war and die for him. These are the ghostly soldiers marching beside me at the grounds.

The rally grounds are a grand illusion. That quality, combined with the weight of their physicality, makes me feel disconnected, not only in my mind but in what I see before me. Sigmund Freud would have termed it 'a moment of derealisation' where the stunned viewer acknowledges, 'So all this really does exist, just as we learnt at school!'[5]

As I walk towards the Zeppelin Field, nature asserts a gentle, persistent presence—green, growing, subtle, flowing. Nature helps me focus, literally, as I photograph its casual and exquisite touches. Grasses which nudge their way between the abandoned stones at the front of the documentation centre. Wildflowers that bloom in the interstices of the steps at the Luitpold Arena. Trees, their branches interwoven, lean close as if in intimate conversation. The lake is broad, laced with reeds, and shimmering with the white and azure reflections of sky and clouds.

I look up. It's an action the architecture forces on the spectator. The immense scale of the buildings, the width of the Great Road, the breadth of the Zeppelin Field, make the eye rise upwards, presumably symbolically, towards the godlike figure of the Führer, the focus of all eyes, of all gazes. Hitler was a small and unattractive man. I've read *Mein Kampf*. It's no more than the ravings of an anti-Semitic lunatic. Looking around, it seems astonishing he could envisage the rally grounds.

Walking towards the grandstand at the Zeppelin Field, I see that building works are underway. It's a relief to see people going about

Nazi Party Rally Grounds, Nuremberg, Janine Burke, 2012.

their jobs, doing something normal in this abnormal place. It's a relief to see anyone at all. The last group of tourists I met up with, who were Japanese, have left. I'm glad I brought a bottle of water. The day is warm and the cafe and toilets are at the other end of the grounds. Some of the workmen look at me with curiosity but it's friendly, as if they want to ask why I'm here.

The grandstand is Speer's grotesque version of the Pergamon Altar. It was there that Hitler announced the 'Final Solution' of the Jewish people. A few days before, I'd been in Berlin's Altes Museum where I saw this spectacular work of art, a monumental construction built around 200 BC, on the acropolis of the ancient city of Pergamon in Turkey. What gives the altar its grandeur is not only its scale but the intense, beautiful and passionate sculptures of the gods, humans and animals which decorate it. Combining expressive faces, dramatic gestures and fluttering draperies, the sculptures form a series of glorious, interlocking movements. Speer reduced an example of the highest human skill and endeavour to a bland, awesomely large stage at whose topmost point a huge swastika was fixed. In 1945, American troops blew up the swastika.

My return journey takes me to the cafe that is opposite the lake. Sitting outside in the balmy air are mothers and kids, families having lunch.

I feel like I've arrived from another planet. At the cafe, there are older people who must have stories and memories of the grounds. In the 1950s, the Zeppelin Field was used for motorcycle races. In 1967, a section of the grandstand was detonated due to its dilapidation. For decades the people of Nuremberg struggled with what to do with the rally grounds. At that time, Germany hid from its history until it was prompted, as Berlin has done, to expose its worst features, to examine both fact and psyche.

A few weeks later, I return to Melbourne and begin to work on the photographs, the long process of sifting and selecting images.

To my dismay, I find the rally grounds have defeated me. The lovely whispering trees look like shadowy conspirators. The man at the lake seems suspicious. Was that his granddaughter? Why was he there with that child? The duck's pale feather appears timid. A breeze could blow it away. The sky is as hostile as a glare. The clouds are filled with rain. The grace notes I'd sought to introduce are insubstantial against the scale and heft of the stones, the massive, resonant emptiness. The rally grounds are saturated with horror. It's poisoned and nothing can change that, not even the magical charms of nature.

Epilogue

I THINK IT'S APPROPRIATE to end where we began—in Elwood. It's spring and gusty northerlies are swirling through the suburb. The trees and bushes have bloomed, providing a heady mixture of beauty and perfume—pink and white blossom trees whose artful architecture inspired Monet and Van Gogh, divinely sensual Tulip Magnolias (*Magnolia soulangeana*), several types of Wattle, Common Jasmine (*Jasminum officinale*) which decks fences in sweet-smelling riot, flawless Camellias and my absolute favourite, Pittosporum (*Pittosporum undulatum*) whose scent makes me fairly swoon with pleasure.

Though one must be careful. The bees are harvesting these flowering plants, so before you (literally) stick your nose in, make sure you allow the bees precedence. I learned the hard way. Delighting in the rich, creamy scent of a rose, my stickybeak disturbed Ms Bee who was cross and buzzed at me. Go away, clumsy human! I'm busy!

The sewerage-devouring Plane at the front of my block is hosting a Magpie Lark couple who are building their mud nest on one of its branches, frantically fast. It's the busiest time of the year for the birds. There's also the ceaseless chirruping of Noisy Miner babies, demanding food. Their parents are so organised and responsible, I can't help but admire their energy and commitment as they dive on grubs, then zoom back to the nest to feed the little ones.

My apartment has also turned into a tree, offering nurseries and accommodation. In the air vent in my study, a family of Mynas has established itself. I hear the babies calling for food and the sudden silence when it's delivered. A King Parrot family inhabit part of my bedroom ceiling. The parents managed to peck a small entrance via the roof beam. I watched them do it, as I sat on the balcony at sunset, work over for the day, sipping a glass of wine. I suppose I should have been annoyed. Now I'm sleeping with earplugs so as not to be awoken at dawn.

I must admit I've formed something of a bond with the Sugar Gum and visit it most days. I just sit there without expectation. Perhaps Monica Gagliano is right and once you connect with a tree, it will communicate with you for the rest of your life. I'm happy to wait. Patience is a virtue I aspire to. Though it's always fun when the Cockatoos arrive. They're usually up to tricks. I've learned that One-eye is not only the largest and loudest of the Sugar Gum Cockatoo cohort, he's the boss. When I hear the most raucous screeching across the suburb, I know it's him, flying off to forage or heading home with the rest of the gang.

There's also my old friend the European Ash on Elster Creek, which is looking magnificent in the full glory of its green attire.

I realise I could write this book forever. There's always another tree to discover, to study, to admire. Another myth, another story, another history. Another work of art. Another journey, more travels of the mind, of the body.

These are my forests, based on my tree experiences. You might have your own. Perhaps many of us nurture, deep within our memories, secret forests, trees associated with our childhood, our adventures, our gardens, trees that flourish still. Elwood helped me to learn what a forest is, what it can be. It takes time, it takes decades. I feel I've only just begun. So here I abide.

Long after I'm gone, I fancy my spirit will still be walking, along Elster Creek, past the Sugar Gum and the Ash, onward to the sea.

Notes

Elwood, My Forest

1 Oliver Wendell Holmes, *The Autocrat of the Breakfast-Table*, 1858. *The Autocrat of the Breakfast-Table* was printed in monthly instalments in *Atlantic Monthly*, November 1857 – October 1858. The online edition is the first book edition: Phillips, Sampson and Company, Boston, 1861. https://www.gutenberg.org/files/751/751-h/751-h. htm. Retrieved 5 February 2020.

2 In 1974, a midden was recorded in the vicinity of Point Ormond, during the redevelopment of the junction at Barkly Street, Glen Huntly Road and Ormond Esplanade. Middens are former cooking sites containing charcoal, shells, bone and stone flints. Stone axes were also recovered from the area. Meyer Eidelson, *Yalukit Willam: The river people of Port Phillip*, City of Port Phillip, St Kilda, 2014, p. 8.

3 'The name *Yaluk-ut Weelam Ngargee* was gifted by N'arweet Carolyn Briggs, Chairperson of the Boonwurrung Foundation, and loosely means "People, Place, Gathering".' Yaluk-ut Weelam Festival. https://www.ywnf.com.au/festival-info/about-yaluk-ut-weelam-ngargee. Retrieved 20 October 2020. See also Ian D Clark, *The Yalukit-Willam: The First People of Hobsons Bay*, Hobsons Bay Library, Hobsons Bay, 2011, p. 1. https://libraries.hobsonsbay.vic.gov.au/component/content/article/23-discover/hobsons-bay-history-indigenous/92-indigenous-history. Retrieved 11 May 2017.

4 Earthcare, in partnership with the City of Port Phillip, began planting Elwood intensively from 1989 onward including many varieties of local indigenous plants. The plantings are maintained by the City of Port Phillip. Meyer Eidelson. Email to the author. 11 March 2020.

5 Sydney Parkinson. Quoted in Bill Gammage, *The Biggest Estate on Earth: How Aborigines made Australia*, Allen and Unwin, Sydney, 2012, p. 5.

6 Meyer Eidelson, *Yalukit William*, p. 13.

7 John McPhee, *The Art of John Glover*, Macmillan, Melbourne, 1980, p. 30. McPhee believes Glover's words, quoted by George Augustus Robinson, were on a piece of paper attached to the back of a Glover painting and the painting has since been re-lined. Email to the author. 18 April 2020.

8 I am grateful to Professor Lyndall Ryan, University of Newcastle, for providing this information. Email to the author. 19 April 2020.

9 Lyndall Ryan presents an 'against the grain' reading of Batman's treaty with Aboriginal leaders including Derrimut and Billibellary. The conventional view has been that Batman was engaged in a land grab and that Aboriginal people were naively unaware of the repercussions of the treaty. See Lyndall Ryan, 'Billibellary, the Formation of the Native Police Force in the Port Phillip District in 1837 and Its Connection to the Batman Treaty of 1835', *Law and History*, vol. 4, no. 2, 2017, pp. 4–6.

10 Meyer Eidelson, *Yalukit Willam*, p. 53.

11 Richard Broome, *Aboriginal Victorians: A history since 1800*, Allen and Unwin, Sydney, 2005, p. 29.

12 Meyer Eidelson, *Yalukit Willam*, p. 54.

13 Marguerita Stephens (ed.), *The Journal of William Thomas: Assistant protector of the Aborigines of Port Phillip and guardian of the Aborigines of Victoria 1839 to 1867*, 19 November 1860, Victorian Aboriginal Corporation for Languages, Melbourne, vol. 111, 2014, p. 288.

14 The Ngargee Tree, St Kilda Swamp (Albert Park Reserve). The St Kilda Ngargee or Corroboree Tree is located in the south-east corner of Albert Park between Albert Park Lake and Fitzroy Street at St Kilda Junction. It is marked by a wooden plaque reading, 'This red gum eucalypt known as the "Corroboree" or "Ngargee" Tree is estimated to be 300–500 years old. It is believed to mark the site of Aboriginal ceremonies held prior to European settlement in 1835. The tree is a symbol of the cultural heritage of the original Australians.'

15 Meyer Eidelson, *Yalukit Willam*, p. 34.

16 Recorded interview with Meyer Eidelson, 11 February 2020, Middle Park, Victoria.

17 Peter Wohlleben, *The Hidden Life of Trees: What they feel, how they communicate—Discoveries from a secret world*, Black Inc., Carlton, 2016, p. 83.

18 Patrick Baker. Email to the author. 31 May 2017.

19 Andy Coghlan, 'Trees Seen Resting Branches while "Asleep" for the First Time', *New Scientist*, 18 May 2016. https://www.newscientist.com/article/2088833-trees-seen-resting-branches-while-asleep-for the first time. Retrieved 10 February 2020.

Trees as Home

1 The Institute of Human Origins, Arizona State University, Tempe, has replicas of Lucy's bones, which were produced in the institute's casting and moulding laboratories. 'The "real" Lucy is stored in a specially constructed safe in the Paleoanthropology Laboratories, National Museum of Ethiopia, Addis Ababa. Because of the rare and fragile nature of many fossils, including hominins, moulds are often made of the original fossils. The moulds are then used to create detailed casts which can be used for teaching, research and exhibitions.' https://iho.asu.edu/about/lucys-story. Retrieved 7 September 2020.

2 Author Unknown, 'Six Million Years of African Savanna', National Science Foundation, 3 August 2011. https://www.nsf.gov/news/news_summ.jsp?cntn_id=121029. Retrieved 19 February 2020.

3 Wattieza is extinct like Archaeopteris, the previous contender for the first tree title. Archaeopteris has living relatives including the Conifer, which gives a clue to its name, First Wing (*Archaeo*: first, *pteris*: wing, due to its feathery leaves). In the Late Devonian (380–360 million years ago), Archaeopteris ruled the world, making up 90 per cent of its forests. Like Wattieza, it shed spores to reproduce, just as ferns, algae and fungi do, but unlike Wattieza, it had wide branches and a canopy of leaves. In time, Archaeopteris rotted. The moulds of the stumps left in the sand were eventually filled with more sand, leaving the tree-stump fossils. In 1850, an amateur naturalist found a sandstone cast of a portion of a Devonian-age tree trunk in Schoharie Creek near Gilboa, New York State, after a huge flood. The samples were sent to Canada where the specimens were described and illustrated by McGill University palaeontologist John W Dawson. It was the first documented discovery of fossil tree stumps in North America. See https://www.gilboafossils.org. Retrieved 17 January 2017.

4 Ker Than, 'World's First Tree Reconstructed', *Live Science*, 18 April 2007. http://www.livescience.com/1439-world-tree-reconstructed.html. Retrieved 19 February 2020.

5 Tim Flannery, *Here on Earth: An argument for hope*, Text Publishing, Melbourne, 2010, p. 196.

6 Scott Cane, *First Footprints: The epic story of the First Australians*, Allen and Unwin, Sydney, 2013, p. viii.

7 In 2011, BBCTV filmed the Korowai building a treehouse for the documentary series *Human Planet*. But the vastly high treehouse, spectacular to behold, was a fake. The build was staged, earning the BBC censure. Mark Sweney, 'BBC admits treehouse scene from Human Planet series was faked', 4 April 2018, https://www.theguardian.com/media/2018/apr/04/scene-from-human-planet-documentary-was-faked-bbc-admits. Retrieved 7 September 2020.

8 Gerrit J van Enk and Lourens de Vries, *The Korowai of Irian Jaya: Their language in its cultural context*, Oxford University Press, Oxford, 1997, p. 23.

9 Rupert Stasch, 'Korowai Treehouses and the Everyday Representation of Time, Belonging and Death', *The Asia Pacific Journal of Anthropology*, vol. 12, no. 4, August 2011, p. 327.

10 Gerrit J van Enk and Lourens de Vries, *The Korowai of Irian Jaya*, p. 22.

11 Paul Raffaele, 'Sleeping with Cannibals', *Smithsonian Magazine*, September 2006. http://www.smithsonianmag.com/travel/sleeping-with-cannibals-128958913/#yDsEb2tgEkajeOHD.99. Retrieved 19 February 2020.

12 ibid.

13 ibid.

14 The Observer Tree. https://observertree.org/about/. Retrieved 9 September 2020.

15 Recorded interview with Miranda Gibson, 10 August 2017, Elwood, Victoria.

16 ibid.

17 *Miranda Gibson*. A film by Jeff Wirth, 2014. https://www.youtube.com/watch?v=Q26PNqyxIm4. Retrieved 27 July 2017.

18 ibid.

19 Recorded interview with Miranda Gibson, 10 August 2017, Elwood, Victoria.

20 Miranda Gibson, 'I Spent 449 Days in a Tree Without Touching the Ground—It Was All Worth It', *The Guardian*, 25 June 2013. https://www.theguardian.com/commentisfree/2013/jun/25/tasmania-tree-protest-logging. Retrieved 7 September 2020.

21 ibid.

22 ibid.

23 Recorded interview with Miranda Gibson, 10 August 2017, Elwood, Victoria.

24 ibid.

25 Peter Wohlleben, *The Hidden Life of Trees: What they feel, how they communicate—Discoveries from a secret world*, Black Inc., Carlton, 2016, p. 83.

26 Daniel Chamovitz, *What a Plant Knows: A field guide to the senses*, Scribe Publications, Melbourne, 2012, p. 9.

27 ibid., p. 128.

Gardens of Eden

1 Quoted in Michael Molnar, ed. and trans., *The Diary of Sigmund Freud, 1929–1939: A record of the final decade*, Scribner, London, 1992, p. 247.

2 PRJ Ford, *Oriental Carpet Design: A guide to traditional motifs, patterns and symbols*, Thames and Hudson, London, 1981, p. 122.

3 ibid., p. 110.

4 Jane Brown, *Gardens of a Golden Afternoon: A social history of gardens and gardening*, Penguin, Harmondsworth, 1985, p. 34.

5 Margereta Tengberg, 'Beginnings and Early History of Date Palm Garden Cultivation in the Middle East', *Journal of Arid Environments*, vol. 86, November 2012, pp. 139–47. https://www.sciencedirect.com/science/article/pii/S0140196311003569#!. Retrieved 8 September 2020.

6 Walter Boelich (ed.), *The Letters of Sigmund Freud to Eduard Silberstein, 1871–1881*, trans. Arnold Pomerans, Harvard University Press, Cambridge, 1990, pp. 33–6.

7 Sigmund Freud, 'Screen Memories', (1899), *The Standard Edition of the Complete Psychological Works of Sigmund Freud*, in James Strachey (ed. and trans.) in collaboration with Anna Freud, The Hogarth Press, London, 1974, vol. III, p. 312. While Freud attributed these memories to a patient, they are, his editors believe, his own.

8 ibid.

9 Ernest Jones, *The Life and Work of Sigmund Freud*, Basic Books, New York, 1953–57, vol. II, p. 99.

10 Martin Freud, *Glory Reflected: Sigmund Freud—man and father*, Angus and Robertson, London, 1957, p. 59.

11 Pamela Norris, *The Story of Eve*, Picador, London, 1998, p. 2.

12 Roger Deakin, *Wildwood: A journey through trees*, Hamish Hamilton, London, 2006, p. 285.

13 See Barrie E Juniper and David J Mabberley, *The Story of the Apple*, Timber Press, Portland, Oregon, and London, 2006.

Trees of Jesus

1 Ed Cumming, 'Who Will Save the Frankincense Tree?', *Daily Telegraph*, 23 December 2012. http://www.telegraph.co.uk/gardening/gardeningadvice/9758581/What-will-save-the-frankincense-tree.html. Retrieved 20 February 2020.

2 Frans Bongers et al., 'Frankincense in Peril', *Nature Sustainability*, vol. 2, 2019, pp. 602–10. Retrieved 20 February 2020.

3 Charles Dickens, 'Old Lamps for New Ones', *Household Words*, no. 12, 15 June 1850, pp. 12–14. From http://www.engl.duq.edu/servus/PR_Critic/HW15jun50.html. Cited in https://en.wikipedia.org/wiki/Christ_in_the_House_of_His_Parents. Retrieved 20 February 2020.

4 Author Unknown, 'Jerusalem Olive Trees Among Oldest in the World', *ABC News*, 10 October 2012. https://www.abc.net.au/news/2012-10-20/jerusalem-olive-trees-among-oldest-in-world/4324342. Retrieved 20 April 2020. See also Mauro Bernabei, 'The Age of the Olive Trees in the Garden of Gethsemane', *Journal of Archaeological Science*, no. 53, 2015, pp. 43–8. https://www.academia.edu/10259906/The_age_of_the_olive_trees_in_the_Garden_of_Gethsemane. Retrieved 13 April 2020.

5 James Frazer, *The Golden Bough: A study in magic and religion*, Wordsworth Editions, Hertfordshire, UK, 1993, p. 339. This edition was abridged by Frazer from his twelve-volume opus and published in 1922.

6 ibid., p. 345.

7 James Frazer, *Adonis, Attis, Osiris: Studies in the history of oriental religion*, Macmillan, London, 1907, p. 214.

8 Rachel Feltman, 'This Tree Might Be the Oldest Living Thing in Europe', *The Washington Post*, 19 August 2016. https://www.washingtonpost.com/news/speaking-of-science/wp/2016/08/19/this-tree-might-be-the-oldest-living-thing-in-europe/. Retrieved 13 April 2020.

9 ibid.

10 James Frazer, *The Golden Bough*, pp. 348–9.

11 ibid. Frazer also makes the point that the festival of Christmas was borrowed from Mithraism. Mithra was a sun god, known as the Sun of Righteousness, and 25 December, reckoned as the winter solstice (Latin: *sol + stice*, sun standing still), was celebrated as the Nativity of the Sun. It's the shortest/darkest day and from then on the light begins to increase. The Gospels make no comment as to the day of Christ's birth and accordingly the early Church did not celebrate it. It took until around the fourth century AD for Christianity to adopt the date as the Nativity. James Frazer, *Adonis, Attis, Osiris*, pp. 254–5.

12 Amanda Hoh, 'Christmas Tree Farmer Braces for the Silly Season and Offers Tips to Make Your Tree Last', *ABC News*, 5 December 2016. http://www.abc.net.au/news/2016-12-05/how-to-take-care-of-your-christmas-tree/8092810. Retrieved 19 June 2017.

13 Michael Balter, 'Trees Survived Ice Age Chill in Scandinavia', *Science*, 1 March 2012. http://www.sciencemag.org/news/2012/03/trees-survived-ice-age-chill-scandinavia. Retrieved 8 June 2017.

14 Rasmus Kragh Jakobsen, 'Trees Survived the Ice Age in Scandinavia', *ScienceNordic*, 2 March 2012. http://sciencenordic.com/trees-survived-ice-age-scandinavia. Retrieved 8 June 2017.

15 Pines mostly have the male and female cones on the same tree. The male cones are small, typically 1 to 5 centimetres long, and only present for a short period (usually in spring, though autumn in a few Pines), falling as soon as they have shed their pollen. The female cones take one and a half to three years (depending on their species) to mature after pollination. Each cone has numerous spirally arranged scales, with two seeds on each fertile scale; the scales at the base and tip of the cone are small and sterile, without seeds. The seeds are mostly small and winged, and are wind-dispersed, but some are larger and have only a vestigial wing, and are bird-dispersed. At maturity, the cones usually open to release the seeds. In other Pines, the seeds are stored in closed cones for many years until an environmental cue, such as a forest fire, triggers the cones to open, releasing the seeds. John Woloch, 'The Differences between Male Pollen & Female Seed Pine Cones', *Sciencing*, 7 May 2018. https://sciencing.com/differences-female-seed-pine-cones-8094513.html. Retrieved 8 September 2020.

Tree Worshippers

1 Kim D Coder, University of Georgia, 'Falling Tree Leaves: Leaf abscission' (PDF), 1999. http://www.walterreeves.com/uploads/pdf/fallingtreeleavesleafabscission.pdf. Retrieved 9 September 2020.

2 William Carlos Williams, 'Winter Trees', 1921. https://www.poets.org/poetsorg/poem/winter-trees. Retrieved 20 October 2018. Online text copyright © 2003, Ian Lancashire for the Department of English, University of Toronto. Published by the Web Development Group, Information Technology Services, University of Toronto Libraries.

3 *The Poetic Edda*, Henry Adams Bellows (trans.), 1936. https://archive.org/stream/poeticedda00belluoft/poeticedda00belluoft_djvu.txt. Retrieved 22 August 2018.

4 *Völuspá: The Seeress's Prophecy*, Nick Richardson (trans.), 2014. http://thejunket.org/2014/01/archive/voluspa-the-seeresss-prophecy/. Retrieved 20 October 2018.

5 *The Codex Regius*, (*The Poetic Edda*). http://www.germanicmythology.com/works/CODEXREGIUS.html. Retrieved 20 October 2018.

6 In his introductory note to his 1936 translation of *The Poetic Edda*, Henry Adams Bellows comments, 'the first volume [of *The Poetic Edda*] is Voluspa [The Prophecy of Volva], [*sic*] the most famous and important, as it is likewise the most debated, of all the Eddic poems'. The general plan of the Völuspá is 'fairly clear. Othin [Odin], chief of the gods, always conscious of impending disaster and eager for knowledge, calls on a certain "Volva", or wise-woman, presumably bidding her rise from the grave. She first tells him of the past, of the creation of the world, the beginning of years, the origin of the dwarfs … of the first man and woman, of the world-Ash Yggdrasil … she then turns to the real prophesy, the disclosure of the final destruction of the gods'. This battle, in which fire and flood overwhelm heaven and Earth as the gods fight with their enemies, 'is the great fact in Norse mythology'. https://archive.org/stream/poeticedda00belluoft/poeticedda00belluoft_djvu.txt. Retrieved 22 August 2018.

7 Hel (not Hela) is a Norse goddess who, fittingly for her name, rules the underworld. In Norse myth, she was not the sister of Thor.

8 Melissa Breyer, 'Vikings Cleared the Forests, Now Iceland Is Bringing Them Back', *Tree Hugger*, 11 October 2018. If you follow the link, you will find the video where Þröstur Eysteinsson discusses the re-greening of Iceland. https://www.treehugger. com/conservation/vikings-cleared-forests-now-iceland-finally-growing-new-ones. html. Retrieved 9 September 2020.

9 There's a theory that 'Ash' is a mistranslation and that Yggdrasil is actually a Yew. There is some credit to this theory as Yggdrasil is said to be evergreen, as the Conifer Yew is, while differing species of Ash are wholly or sometimes partly deciduous. However, I'm circumspect due to the first man being named Ask, which underpins his symbolic relationship with Yggdrasil and the use of the word ask for the Ash in the original text of *The Poetic Edda*. Visit this link for an imaginative argument in favour of the Yew: Tyra Alrune Sahsnotasvriunt, 'Yggdrasil—Yew not Ash Tree'. https://paganmeltingpot.wordpress.com/2014/09/17/yggdrasil-yew-not-Ash-tree/. Retrieved 9 September 2020.

10 Author Unknown, 'A Seeress from Fyrkat?', National Museum of Denmark. https:// en.natmus.dk/historical-knowledge/denmark/prehistoric-period-until-1050-ad/ the-viking-age/religion-magic-death-and-rituals/a-seeress-from-fyrkat/. Retrieved 9 September 2020.

11 Gavin Haines, 'How Iceland Re-created a Viking-Age Religion', *BBC Travel*, 3 June 2019. http://www.bbc.com/travel/story/20190602-how-iceland-recreated-a-viking-age-religion. Retrieved 9 September 2020.

12 Liv Siddal, 'Spiritual Dimensions—A Visit to the Site of Iceland's New Pagan Temple', 1 June 2015. https://www.itsnicethat.com/articles/iceland-pagan-temple. Retrieved 9 September 2020.

13 By the nineteenth century, linguists knew that all modern Indo-European languages descended from a single tongue. In 1868, German linguist August Schleicher used reconstructed Proto-Indo-European vocabulary to create a fable in order to hear some approximation of PIE. Called 'The Sheep and the Horses', and also known today as 'Schleicher's Fable', it tells the story of a sheep who encounters an unfriendly group of horses. As linguists have continued to discover more about PIE, this sonic experiment continues and the fable is periodically updated to reflect the most current understanding of how this extinct language would have sounded when it was spoken some six thousand years ago. Since there is considerable disagreement among scholars about PIE, no single version can be considered definitive. At the following site, University of Kentucky linguist Andrew Byrd recites his version of the fable, using pronunciation informed by the latest insights into reconstructed PIE: Eric A Powell, 'Telling Tales in Proto-Indo-European', *Archaeology*, n.d. https://www.archaeology.org/exclusives/ articles/1302-proto-indo-european-schleichers-fable. Retrieved 9 September 2020.

Naming Trees

1 There is some confusion about the area Cook named Moreton Bay. In fact, he named the shallow bight between Cape Moreton and North Stradbroke Island, Moreton Bay. On his chart, Cook named the area now known as Moreton Bay, Glasshouse Bay, due to the view he gained of the Glasshouse Mountains (which he also named) from there. Cook did not land in the area nor did he sail further into Moreton Bay. See Ray Parkin, *HM Bark* Endeavour: *Her place in Australian history*, Miegunyah Press, Carlton, 1997, p. 226. It was Matthew Flinders who, in 1799, renamed Glasshouse Bay, Moreton Bay.

2 Christine Peacock, *History, Life and Times of Robert Anderson, Gheebelum, Ngugi, Mulgumpin*, Uniikup Productions, South Brisbane, 2001, p. 20, online.

3 Quoted in JG Steele, *The Explorers of Moreton Bay 1770–1830*, University of Queensland Press, St Lucia, 1983, p. 28.

4 ibid., cedar 'of a fine Grain', p. 21; 'very pretty' wooded islands, p. 23; 'large and luxuriant trees', p. 21.

5 I'm grateful to Dr Dale Dixon, collections manager, Royal Botanic Gardens and Domain Trust, Brisbane, for information about Desfontaines's and Persoon's differing roles in naming and describing *Ficus macrophylla*. Email to the author. 13 January 2014.

6 Christiaan Hendrik Persoon, *Synopsis plantarum, seu Enchiridium botanicum: complectens enumerationem systematicam specierum hucusque cognitarum*, JG Cottam, Paris, 1806, vol. 2, p. 609.

7 Author Unknown, 'Christian Hendrik Persoon. Biographical note'. http://www.mushroomthejournal.com/greatlakesdata/Authors/Persoon21.html. Retrieved 10 September 2020.

8 M. [*sic*] Desfontaines, *Tableau de L'École de Botanique du Muséum D'Histoire Naturelle*, JA Brosson, Paris, 1804, p. 209, online.

9 I'm grateful to Dan Kehlman, Plant Identification and Advisory Services, Queensland Herbarium, for finding this reference to Walter Hill. E Vidler, *Our Own Trees: A first book on the Australian forest*, WA Hamer, Melbourne, 1930, p. 44, online.

10 Nina Rønsted, George D Weiblen, V Savolainen and James M Cook, 'Phylogeny, Biogeography and Ecology of Ficus Section Malvanthera (Moraceae)', *Molecular Phylogenetics and Evolution*, vol. 48, no. 1, 2008, p. 21, online.

11 Jeff Ollerton, 'Biological Barter: Patterns of specialisation compared across different mutualisms', Nickolas M Waser and Jeff Ollerton (eds.) *Plant-Pollinator Interactions: From specialization to generalization*, University of Chicago Press, 2006, p. 411, online. Each species of Fig has its exclusive species of wasp and both are engaged in each other's survival. The Moreton Bay Fig is a hermaphrodite: it has evolved fruit which is both male and female, but they mature at different times. The wasp clambers into the female fruit, a fleshy cup which is known as a syncomium. Then she deposits her eggs and they grow by feeding on it. When her offspring hatch, they mate. The new generation of females then collects pollen from the male fruit, which is mature by then, and visits other female fruit to repeat the process. The wasps are tiny: she's around 3 millimetres long, while her male counterpart is around 1 millimetre. In the right environment, a Moreton Bay Fig can live for several hundred years, so biological barter seems to be working well.

Knowing Trees

1 Sigmund Freud, 'Mourning and Melancholia', (1917), *The Standard Edition of the Complete Psychological Works of Sigmund Freud*, in James Strachey (ed. and trans.) in collaboration with Anna Freud, The Hogarth Press, London, 1957, vol. XIV, p. 255.

2 Part of this chapter was originally published in Janine Burke, *Source: Nature's healing role in art and writing*, Allen and Unwin, Sydney, 2009.

3 Janine Burke, *Second Sight*, Greenhouse Publications, Melbourne, 1986, p. 90.

4 Virginia Woolf, *To the Lighthouse*, The Hogarth Press, London, 1927, p. 237.

5 Ceri Richards, *The Red Skirt*, 1948, Private Collection. Frances Richards, Ceri's wife, and also an artist, is the subject of the painting.

6 Virginia Woolf, 'Modern Fiction', in Andrew McNeillie (ed.), *The Essays of Virginia Woolf*, The Hogarth Press, London, 1984, vol. 4: 1925–1928, p. 160.

7 Virginia Woolf, 'Evening over Sussex: Reflections in a motor car', *The Death of the Moth and Other Essays*, The Hogarth Press, London, 1942, p. 120.

8 Virginia Woolf, 'A Sketch of the Past', in Jeanne Schulkind (ed.), *Virginia Woolf, Moments of Being, Unpublished Autobiographical Writings*, The Hogarth Press, London, 1985, p. 133.

9 Virginia Woolf to Katharine Arnold-Forster, 12 August [1919], in Nigel Nicholson and Joanne Trautmann (eds), *The Letters of Virginia Woolf*, The Hogarth Press, London, 1976, vol. 2: 1912–1922, p. 382.

10 18 August 1921, in Anne Olivier Bell and Andrew McNeillie (eds), *The Diary of Virginia Woolf*, The Hogarth Press, London, 1978, vol. 2: 1920–1924, p. 132.

11 Virginia Woolf to Janet Case, 5 January 1920, in Nigel Nicholson and Joanne Trautmann (eds), *The Letters of Virginia Woolf*, vol. 2, p. 415.

12 3 July 1919, in Anne Olivier Bell and Andrew McNeillie (eds), *The Diary of Virginia Woolf*, The Hogarth Press, London, 1977, vol. 1: 1915–1919, pp. 286–7.

13 Victoria Summerly, 'A Retreat of One's Own: Tending to Virginia Woolf's country plot proved a surprising insight into the writer herself', *The Independent*, 19 October 2013. https://www.independent.co.uk/property/gardening/a-retreat-of-ones-own-tending-to-virginia-woolfs-country-plot-proved-a-surprising-insight-into-the-8884225.html. Retrieved 24 February 2020.

14 Jonathan Zoob. Email to the author. 6 October 2008.

15 ibid.

16 'In the Orchard' was first published in *The Criterion* in April 1923 and edited by TS Eliot.

17 Virginia Woolf, 'In the Orchard'. https://lithub.com/in-the-orchard/. Retrieved 10 March 2020.

18 Quoted in Hermione Lee, *Virginia Woolf*, Chatto and Windus, London, 1996, p. 428.

Trees as Victims

1 Bounties were offered for dead Eagles, and large numbers were poisoned or shot— 147 237 in Western Australia between 1928 and 1968, and 162 430 in Queensland between 1951 and 1966. Indirect poisoning through Dingo baits and pesticides continues to be a major hazard. In Tasmania, the Wedge-Tailed Eagle is threatened by habitat loss and deliberate persecution. Melissa Murray, Wedge-Tailed Eagle, Australian National Museum website. https://australian.museum/learn/animals/birds/wedge-tailed-eagle/. Retrieved 20 March 2020.

2 Robyn Davidson, *No Fixed Address: Nomads and the fate of the planet*, Quarterly Essay, no. 24, Black Inc., Melbourne, 2006, pp. 13–14.

3 Ronald M Berndt and Catherine H Berndt, *The Speaking Land: Myth and story in Aboriginal Australia*, Penguin Books, Ringwood, 1989, p. 6.

4 Don Watson, *The Bush: Travels in rural Australia*, Hamish Hamilton, Melbourne, 2016, p. 10.

5 The painting was commissioned by the family of Phillip Parker King in 1880. 'This painting is based on a sketch by Captain Philip [*sic*] Parker King (1791–1856). King accompanied Sir Richard Bourke, Governor of New South Wales, on a visit to the Port Phillip District in early 1837.' Author Unknown, Entry on Joseph Anderson Panton's *Government Residence, Melbourne 1837* (1880), State Library Victoria catalogue. Retrieved 20 March 2020.

6 While the title *Emerald Hill and Sandridge from the Government Domain* (1857) refers to the suburbs of Emerald Hill (now South Melbourne) and Sandridge (now Port Melbourne) 'it is difficult to pinpoint the exact setting for this painting, and although a press report published in *The Argus* in 1935 suggested that Clark's viewpoint was from somewhere near Fitzroy Street, St Kilda, it seems that a location near to the present-day site of Government House is more likely. Construction of the Victoria Barracks, visible in the lower right of the painting, commenced in May 1856, and close examination reveals a train travelling to Sandridge railway station, which opened in September 1854, the first in Australia. The large marshy area behind the remains of a forest in the centre of the painting is the Lagoon, the present-day Albert Park and Lake. In 1875 Judge Thomas A'Beckett, the owner of this painting, displayed

it at the Intercolonial Exhibition held at the Melbourne Public Library, with its present title.' Author Unknown, Entry on Thomas Clark, *Emerald Hill and Sandridge from the Government Domain* (1857), State Library Victoria catalogue. Retrieved 19 March 2020.

7 See 'Elwood, My Forest', p. 5.

8 Sydney Parkinson. Quoted in Bill Gammage, *The Biggest Estate on Earth: How Aborigines made Australia*, Allen and Unwin, Sydney, 2012, p. 5.

9 The photographic print is attributed to George W Priston, made from a negative created by John Hunter Kerr (1821–1874). http://search.slv.vic.gov.au/primo_library/libweb/action/dlDisplay.do?vid=MAIN&search_scope=default_scope&docId=SLV_VOYAGER1666403&fn=permalink. Retrieved 23 June 2017.

10 *Glimpses of Life in Victoria* by A Resident, Introduction by Marguerite Hancock, Miegunyah Press, Carlton, 1996, p. xi. Hancock points out that, while written in the first person, that is, by John Kerr, Frances Kerr was the author of *Glimpses of Life in Victoria* (p. vii).

11 ibid., p. 11.

12 ibid., p. 151.

13 Andrew Sayers, 'Tommy McRae', *Australian Dictionary of Biography*. http://adb.anu.edu.au/biography/mcrae-tommy-13074. Retrieved 10 July 2017.

14 Andrew Sayers, *Aboriginal Artists of the Nineteenth Century*, Oxford University Press, Melbourne, 1994, p. 27.

15 Lyndall Ryan has researched the massacres of Aboriginal people in Eastern Australia, 1788–1960. A massacre is defined as the death of more than six people. Read an article on her research here: https://www.newcastle.edu.au/newsroom/featured-news/mapping-the-massacres-of-australias-colonial-frontier. Retrieved 9 July 2017. Access the Massacre Map and related information here: https://c21ch.newcastle.edu.au/colonialmassacres/. Retrieved 9 July 2017.

16 Quoted in Andrew Sayers, *Aboriginal Artists of the Nineteenth Century*, p. 144, fn 35.

17 ibid., p. 143, fn 5.

18 Scott Cane, *First Footprints: The epic story of the First Australians*, Allen and Unwin, Sydney, 2013, pp. 134–5.

19 ibid., p. 138.

20 ibid.

21 Kathryn M Collins, Owen F Price and Trent D Penman, 'Spatial Patterns of Wildfire Ignitions in South-Eastern Australia', *International Journal of Wildland Fire*, vol. 24, no. 8, 2015, pp. 1098–108. https://doi.org/10.1071/WF15054. Retrieved 16 July 2017.

22 Chloe Hooper, *The Arsonist: A mind on fire*, Hamish Hamilton, Melbourne, 2018, p. 244.

Women of the Banyan

1 Varanasi. https://www.lonelyplanet.com/india/uttar-pradesh/varanasi. Retrieved 25 May 2020.

2 Robert Southey. Quoted in David L Haberman, *People Trees: Worship of trees in northern India*, Oxford University Press, New York, 2013, p. 165.

3 ibid., p. 165.

4 ibid., p. 172.

5 ibid., p. 175.

6 ibid., p. 176.

7 Devdutt Pattanaik, 'When a Man Loves a Woman', 6 January 2019. https://devdutt.com/articles/when-a-man-loves-a-woman/. Retrieved 22 May 2020.

8 Lydia Smith, 'City of Widows: The 38,000 forgotten women of Varanasi', *International Business Times*, 30 June 2015. https://www.ibtimes.co.uk/city-widows-38000-forgotten-women-varanasi-1505560. Retrieved 22 May 2020.

9 Devdutt Pattanaik, 'When a Man Loves a Woman'. Retrieved 22 May 2020.
10 N Narasimhan, 'Beyond Widowhood, for a Life of Fulfilment', *The Hindu*, 10 September 2017. https://www.thehindu.com/opinion/open-page/beyond-widowhood-for-a-life-of-fulfilment/article19651236.ece. Retrieved 26 May 2020.
11 Richard Phillips and Waruna Alahakoon, 'Hindu Chauvinists Block Filming of Deepa Mehta's *Water*', World Socialist Web Site, 12 February 2000. https://www.wsws.org/en/articles/2000/02/film-f12.html. Retrieved 26 May 2020.
12 Geoffrey Macnab, 'Deepa Mehta: A director in deep water—all over again', *The Independent*, 19 May 2006. https://www.independent.co.uk/arts-entertainment/films/features/deepa-mehta-a-director-in-deep-water-all-over-again-478731.html. Retrieved 26 May 2020.
13 Richard Phillips and Waruna Alahakoon, 'Hindu Chauvinists Block Filming of Deepa Mehta's *Water*'. Retrieved 26 May 2020.
14 Geoffrey Macnab, 'Deepa Mehta: A director in deep water—all over again'. Retrieved 26 May 2020.
15 Lydia Smith, 'City of Widows: The 38,000 forgotten women of Varanasi'. Retrieved 22 May 2020.
16 Kirti Pandey, 'How to Do Vat Savitri Puja', *Times Now News*, 22 May 2020. https://www.timesnownews.com/spiritual/religion/article/how-to-do-vat-savitri-puja-pooja-procedure-vat-savitri-vrat-katha/594380. Retrieved 22 May 2020.

Fairy-tale Forests
1 Bruno Bettelheim, *The Uses of Enchantment: The meaning and importance of fairy tales*, Thames and Hudson, London, 1976.
2 Jim Robbins, 'Chronicles of the Rings: What trees tell us', *The New York Times*, 30 April 2019. https://www.nytimes.com/2019/04/30/science/tree-rings-climate.html. Retrieved 9 June 2020.
3 Dendrochronology. *Dendro*, New Latin from the Greek *dendron*, tree. *Chronos*, Greek, time. *–logy*, Medieval Latin, study of a particular subject. New technologies and techniques are able to pry a much deeper and wider range of information out of trees. There are now roughly a dozen large laboratories globally and data from 4000 sites on all continents except Antarctica. The information is stored in the International Tree-Ring Data Bank, a library open to all researchers. See International Tree-Ring Data Bank, National Centers for Environmental Information, National Oceanic and Atmospheric Administration, Asheville, North Carolina, United States. https://www.ncdc.noaa.gov/data-access/paleoclimatology-data/datasets/tree-ring. Retrieved 9 June 2020.
4 Rachel Kent, 'After Nature', in Rachel Kent (ed.), *Janet Laurence After Nature*, Museum of Contemporary Art Australia, Sydney, 2019, p. 44.
5 Quoted in Rachel Kent, 'After Nature', p. 45.
6 Matt Sendy, '"The Amazon is Completely Lawless": The rainforest after Bolsonaro's first year', *The New York Times*, 5 December 2019. https://www.nytimes.com/2019/12/05/world/americas/amazon-fires-bolsonaro-photos.html. Retrieved 8 June 2020.
7 ibid.
8 Ernesto Londoño, Manuela Andreon and Letícia Casado, 'Amazon Deforestation Soars as Pandemic Hobbles Enforcement', *The New York Times*, 6 June 2020. https://www.nytimes.com/2020/06/06/world/americas/amazon-deforestation-brazil.html. Retrieved 8 June 2020.
9 ibid.
10 Quoted in Rachel Kent, 'After Nature', p. 45.
11 ibid., p. 240.

12 In 1697, Perrault had published *Tales and Stories of the Past with Morals* (*Histoires ou Contes du Temps Passé*), which earned him enormous and ongoing popularity. Lydie Jean comments that the book was 'the biggest success in French literary history. No other book has been as modified, and yet as extensively published and read'. Lydie Jean, 'Charles Perrault's Paradox: How aristocratic fairy tales became synonymous with folklore conservation', *Trames*, vol. 11 (61/56) no. 3, 2007, p. 282. In the same year, Baroness d'Aulnoy published *Fairy Tales* (*Les Contes des Fées*).

13 In Perrault's version of *Little Red Riding Hood*, she takes off her clothes and gets into bed with the Wolf. She's then eaten alive. There's no happy ending as in the Brothers Grimm. In 1862, Gustave Doré published an illustrated volume of Perrault's tales. The work in the collection of the National Gallery of Victoria indicates Perrault was so compelled by the story he recast it as a painting.

14 Bruno Bettelheim, *The Uses of Enchantment*, p. 166.

15 ibid., pp. 5–6.

16 ibid., p. 172.

17 Amy Odell, 'Has PETA Finally Won the War Against Fur?', *The Cut*, 1 October 2018. https://www.thecut.com/2018/10/has-peta-finally-won-the-war-against-fur.html. Retrieved 26 June 2020.

18 Sarah Bonner, 'Visualising Little Red Riding Hood', *Moveable Type*, vol. 2, 'The Mind's Eye', University College, London, 2006. https://discovery.ucl.ac.uk/id/eprint/1572292/1/Sarah%20Bonner.pdf. Retrieved 26 June 2020.

19 Angela Carter, *The Bloody Chamber*, Harper and Row, New York, 1979, p. 143.

20 ibid., p. 147.

21 ibid., p. 148.

22 ibid., p. 150.

23 ibid., p. 150.

24 ibid., p. 153.

25 The Grimms were encouraged to collect folk songs, tales and poems by Romantic poet and writer Clemens Brentano. They began to systematically collect the tales when Brentano asked them to supply oral tales for a book of literary fairy tales he was preparing. With Achim von Arnim (the husband of Bettina von Arnim), Brentano published *Des Knaben Wunderhorn: Alte deutsche Lieder* (*The Boy's Magic Horn: Old German songs*) (1805–08). The brothers contributed research for the book. Between 1807 and 1810, the brothers became more focused on prose tales. During that time, Jacob was the dominating force of the two in terms of collecting and collating the tales. Jack Zipes, *Grimm Legacies: The magic spell of the Grimms' folk and fairy tales*, Princeton University Press, Princeton University, NJ, 2015, p. 14.

26 Jacob and Wilhelm Grimm. Introduction to the second volume of the first edition of *Kinder-und Haus-märchen* (*Children's and Household Tales*) (1815). Quoted in Jack Zipes, *Grimm Legacies*, p. 16.

27 Jack Zipes, *Grimm Legacies*, p. 14.

Sentience

1 Tim Flannery, *Here on Earth: An argument for hope*, Text Publishing, Melbourne, 2010, p. 34.

2 James Lovelock, *Revenge of Gaia: Earth's climate crisis and the fate of humanity*, Westview Press, Boulder, 2007, p. 162.

3 Ilima Loomis, 'Trees in the Amazon Make Their Own Rain', *Science*, 4 August 2017. https://www.sciencemag.org/news/2017/08/trees-amazon-make-their-own-rain. Retrieved 15 July 2020.

4 Monica Gagliano, *Thus Spoke the Plant: A remarkable journey of groundbreaking scientific discoveries and personal encounters with plants*, North Atlantic Books, Berkeley, 2018, p. 45.

5 ibid., p. 10.
6 ibid.
7 Snigdha Das, 'Plants Have a Lot More than Five Senses', *Nagaland Today,* 3 January 2019. https://nagalandtoday.in/news/2019/01/plants-have-a-lot-more-than-five-senses/. Retrieved 20 July 2020.
8 Monica Gagliano, *Thus Spoke the Plant*, p. 14.
9 Author Unknown, 'Ayahuasca', Alcohol and Drug Foundation, 18 May 2020. https://adf.org.au/drug-facts/ayahuasca/. Retrieved 21 July 2020.
10 Sean Illing, 'The Brutal Mirror: What the psychedelic drug ayahuasca showed me about my life', first published 19 February 2018. https://www.vox.com/first-person/2018/2/19/16739386/ayahuasca-retreat-psychedelic-hallucination-meditation. Retrieved 21 July 2020. None of the shamans who facilitated the ceremony in Costa Rica that Illing attended were South American Indigenous people. Some were American or Israeli. In his essay, Illing describes the ritual of drinking the potion over several nights with a group of people at the retreat. While the physical results included vomiting and nausea, he felt the discomfort was outweighed by the emotional and psychological benefits, mainly a feeling of connection with others and a rekindling of his love for his wife.
11 Monica Gagliano, *Thus Spoke the Plant*, p. 14.
12 Monica Gagliano, www.youtube.com/watch?v=90BUQoLu_Hg. 26 November 2018. Retrieved 23 July 2020.
13 Leslie Taylor, 'Bellaco Caspi', *Rain-Tree Publishers*. https://rain-tree.com/himatanthus.htm. Retrieved 23 July 2020.
14 Peter Wohlleben, *The Hidden Life of Trees: What they feel, how they communicate—Discoveries from a Secret World*, Black Inc., Carlton, 2016, p. 230.
15 Charles Darwin to Sir Joseph Hooker, 25 March 1878, in Francis Darwin (ed.), *Life and Letters of Charles Darwin*, Basic Books, New York, 1959, vol. II, p. 503. Quoted in Wikipedia entry on *The Power of Movement in Plants*. https://en.wikipedia.org/wiki/The_Power_of_Movement_in_Plants. Retrieved 5 August 2020.
16 Charles Darwin, *The Descent of Man and Selection in Relation to Sex* (1879), Introduction by James Moore and Adrian Desmond, Penguin Books, London, 2004, p. 465.
17 Magpie Larks B31719 (Museum of Victoria catalogue number)
Grallina cyanoleuca
Materials: Cup shaped bowl of plant fibre bound with mud. Lined with grasses, tendrils and leaf fragments.
Built by: Both parents.
Time to build: Can take 7 days to 1 month.
Shape: Cup.
Site: Tree.
Nest diameter: 13.9 cm L x 13.5 cm W.
Nest depth: 8 cm.
Weight: 424 grams. (Weight includes branch to which nest is attached).
Locality: Australia.
Collector/Donor: Unknown.
Magpie Larks are common Australian birds, except in Tasmania. Both males and females have distinctive black and white, pied plumage. Both parents select the nest site, located near water for the process of making the mud for this sturdy nest. It is usually positioned in a Eucalypt on a bare horizontal branch and is sometimes sheltered by foliage or an overhanging branch. Sometimes the Magpie Larks re-use the nest if the first clutch is successful. They make modifications such as expanding the sides of the nest and then relining it. Both incubate and brood the nestlings, taking it in turn to forage for food.

The nest is built from the inside. When building, the bird stands in the middle of the nest and applies mud on the outside, making a 30–60° turn after each application, and occasionally sitting down in the nest to shape it by turning around. The inside of the nest is shaped by a shuffling motion in which one foot is swept back and forth along one side of the nest while the bird pushes its breast along the opposite side, with one outstretched foot for support. Mud is placed on top of the structure and pushed into place with a closed bill, like a cement trowel. When building, distinct layers of progressively wetter material from base to rim can be seen, corresponding to each day of construction.

18 [24 December 1940] Anne Olivier Bell and Andrew McNeillie (eds), *The Diary of Virginia Woolf*, The Hogarth Press, London, 1980, vol. 5, p. 346.

19 Qing Li, *Into the Forest: How trees can help you find health and happiness*, Penguin Random House, London, 2019, p. 5.

20 ibid., p. 117.

21 ME O'Brien, H Anderson, E Kaukel, K O'Byrne, M Pawlicki, J Von Pawel and M Reck, 'SRL172 (Killed Mycobacterium Vaccae) in Addition to Standard Chemotherapy Improves Quality of Life Without Affecting Survival, in Patients with Advanced Non-Small-Cell Lung Cancer: Phase III Results', *PubMed. Gov*, 2004. https://pubmed.ncbi.nlm.nih.gov/15151947/. Retrieved 5 August 2020.

Trees as Witnesses

1 Richard Sexton, *Vestiges of Grandeur: The plantations of Louisiana's River Road*, Chronicle Books, San Francisco, 1999, p. 36.

2 Quoted in Margaret Varnell Clark, *The Louisiana Irish: A historical collation*, iUniverse, New York, 2007, p. 89.

3 Harriet Beecher Stowe, *Uncle Tom's Cabin, or, Life among the Lowly*, John Jewell Brown and Company, Boston, 1852, vol. II, Chapter XXX, 'The Slave Warehouse', n.p., The Project Gutenberg. http://www.gutenberg.org/files/203/203-h/203-h.htm. Retrieved 3 September 2020.

4 Susan Sontag, *On Photography*, Dell Publishing, New York, 1973, p. 119.

5 Sigmund Freud, 'A Disturbance of Memory on the Acropolis' (1936), *The Standard Edition of the Complete Psychological Works of Sigmund Freud*, in James Strachey (ed. and trans.) in collaboration with Anna Freud, The Hogarth Press, London, 1962, vol. XXII, pp. 240–1.

Bibliography

Books

Bell, Anne Olivier and Andrew McNeillie (eds), *The Diary of Virginia Woolf*, vol. 1: 1915–1919, The Hogarth Press, London, 1977.

Bell, Anne Olivier and Andrew McNeillie (eds), *The Diary of Virginia Woolf*, vol. 2: 1920–1924, The Hogarth Press, London, 1978.

Berndt, Ronald M and Catherine H Berndt, *The Speaking Land: Myth and story in Aboriginal Australia*, Penguin Books, Ringwood, 1989.

Bettelheim, Bruno, *The Uses of Enchantment: The meaning and importance of fairy tales*, Thames and Hudson, London, 1976.

Boelich, Walter (ed.) and Arnold Pomerans (trans.), *The Letters of Sigmund Freud to Eduard Silberstein, 1871–1881*, Harvard University Press, Cambridge, 1990.

Broome, Richard, *Aboriginal Victorians: A history since 1800*, Allen and Unwin, Sydney, 2005.

Brown, Jane, *Gardens of a Golden Afternoon: A social history of gardens and gardening*, Penguin, Harmondsworth, 1985.

Burke, Janine, *Second Sight*, Greenhouse Publications, Melbourne, 1986.

Cane, Scott, *First Footprints: The epic story of the First Australians*, Allen and Unwin, Sydney, 2013.

Carter, Angela, *The Bloody Chamber*, Harper and Row, New York, 1979.

Chamovitz, Daniel, *What a Plant Knows: A field guide to the senses*, Scribe Publications, Melbourne, 2012.

Clark, Ian D, *The Yalukit-Willam: The First People of Hobsons Bay*, Hobsons Bay Library, Hobsons Bay, 2011. https://libraries.hobsonsbay.vic.gov.au/component/content/article/23-discover/hobsons-bay-history-indigenous/92-indigenous-history.

Clark, Margaret Varnell, *The Louisiana Irish: A historical collation*, iUniverse, New York, 2007.

Cunningham, Sophie, *City of Trees: Essays on life, death and the need for a forest*, Text Publishing, Melbourne, 2019.

Darwin, Charles, *The Descent of Man and Selection in Relation to Sex* (1879), Introduction by James Moore and Adrian Desmond, Penguin Books, London, 2004.

Darwin, Charles and Francis Darwin (ed.), *The Power of Movement in Plants*, 1880. https://en.wikipedia.org/wiki/The_Power_of_Movement_in_Plants.

Davidson, Robyn, *No Fixed Address: Nomads and the fate of the planet*, Quarterly Essay, no. 24, Black Inc., Melbourne, 2006.

Deakin, Roger, *Wildwood: A journey through trees*, Hamish Hamilton, London, 2006.

Desfontaines, M. [*sic*], *Tableau de L'École de Botanique du Muséum D'Histoire Naturelle*, JA Brosson, Paris, 1804. https://www.biodiversitylibrary.org/bibliography/13828#/summary.

Eidelson, Meyer, *Yalukit Willam: The river people of Port Phillip*, City of Port Phillip, St Kilda, 2014.

Flannery, Tim, *Here on Earth: An argument for hope*, Text Publishing, Melbourne, 2010.

Ford, PRJ, *Oriental Carpet Design: A guide to traditional motifs, patterns and symbols*, Thames and Hudson, London, 1981.

Frazer, James, *Adonis, Attis, Osiris: Studies in the history of oriental religion*, Macmillan, London 1907.

——*The Golden Bough: A study in magic and religion*, Wordsworth Editions, Herefordshire, UK, 1993.

Freud, Martin, *Glory Reflected: Sigmund Freud—man and father*, Angus and Robertson, London, 1957.

Gagliano, Monica, *Thus Spoke the Plant: A remarkable journey of groundbreaking scientific discoveries and personal encounters with plants*, North Atlantic Books, Berkeley, 2018.

Gammage, Bill, *The Biggest Estate on Earth: How Aborigines made Australia*, Allen and Unwin, Sydney, 2012.

Greer, Germaine, *White Beech: The rainforest years*, Bloomsbury, London, 2014.

Grimm, Wilhelm and Jacob Grimm, *The Complete Fairy Tales*, Wordsworth Editions, Ware, Hertfordshire, 1997.

Haberman, David L, *People Trees: Worship of trees in Northern India*, Oxford University Press, New York, 2013.

Holmes, Oliver Wendell, *The Autocrat of the Breakfast-Table*, 1858, online edition Phillips, Sampson and Company, Boston, 1861. https://www.gutenberg.org/files/751/751-h/751-h.htm.

Hooper, Chloe, *The Arsonist: A mind on fire*, Hamish Hamilton, Melbourne, 2018.

Jones, Ernest, *The Life and Work of Sigmund Freud*, vol. II: 1901–1919, Basic Books, New York, 1957.

Juniper, Barrie E and David J Mabberley, *The Story of the Apple*, Timber Press, Portland, Oregon, and London, 2006.

Kerr, John, *Glimpses of Life in Victoria by a Resident*, Introduction by Marguerite Hancock, Miegunyah Press, Carlton, 1996.

Lee, Hermione, *Virginia Woolf*, Chatto and Windus, London, 1996.

Li, Qing, *Into the Forest: How trees can help you find health and happiness*, Penguin Random House, London, 2019.

Lovelock, James, *Revenge of Gaia: Earth's climate crisis and the fate of humanity*, Westview Press, Boulder, 2007.

McNeillie, Andrew (ed.), *The Essays of Virginia Woolf*, vol. 4: 1925–1928, The Hogarth Press, London, 1984.

McPhee, John, *The Art of John Glover*, Macmillan, Melbourne, 1980.

Molnar, Michael (ed. and trans.), *The Diary of Sigmund Freud, 1929–1939: A record of the final decade*, Scribner, London, 1992.

Nicholson, Nigel and Joanne Trautmann (eds), *The Letters of Virginia Woolf*, vol. 2, 1912–1922, The Hogarth Press, London, 1976.

Norris, Pamela, *The Story of Eve*, Picador, London, 1998.

Parkin, Ray, HM Bark Endeavour: *Her place in Australian history*, Miegunyah Press, Carlton, 1997.

Pascoe, Bruce, *Dark Emu: Aboriginal Australia and the birth of agriculture*, Magabala Books, Broome, 2019.

Peacock, Christine, *History, Life and Times of Robert Anderson, Gheebelum, Ngugi, Mulgumpin*, Uniikup Productions, South Brisbane, 2001. https://stradbrokemuseum.com.au/wp-content/uploads/2019/05/bob_anderson_screen_final.pdf.

Persoon, Christiaan Hendrik, *Synopsis plantarum, seu Enchiridium botanicum: complectens enumerationem systematicam specierum hucusque cognitarum*, vol. 2, JG Cottam, Paris, 1806.

Powers, Richard, *The Overstory*, WW Norton and Company, New York, 2018.

Sayers, Andrew, *Aboriginal Artists of the Nineteenth Century*, Oxford University Press, Melbourne, 1994.

Schulkind, Jeanne (ed.), *Virginia Woolf, Moments of Being, Unpublished Autobiographical Writings*, The Hogarth Press, London, 1985.

Sexton, Richard, *Vestiges of Grandeur: The plantations of Louisiana's River Road*, Chronicle Books, San Francisco, 1999.

Steele, JG, *The Explorers of Moreton Bay 1770–1830*, University of Queensland Press, St Lucia, 1983.

Stephens, Marguerita (ed.), *The Journal of William Thomas: Assistant protector of the Aborigines of Port Phillip and guardian of the Aborigines of Victoria 1839 to 1867*, Victorian Aboriginal Corporation for Languages, Melbourne, 2014.

Stowe, Harriet Beecher, *Uncle Tom's Cabin, or, Life among the Lowly*, John Jewell Brown and Company, Boston, 1852. The Project Gutenberg. http://www.gutenberg.org/files/203/203-h/203-htm.

The Codex Regius (The Poetic Edda). http://www.germanicmythology.com/works/CODEXREGIUS.html.

The Poetic Edda, Henry Adams Bellows (trans.), 1936. https://archive.org/stream/poeticedda00belluoft/poeticedda00belluoft_djvu.txt.

Van Enk, Gerrit J, and Lourens de Vries, *The Korowai of Irian Jaya: Their language in its cultural context*, Oxford University Press, Oxford, 1997.

Vidler, E, *Our Own Trees: A first book on the Australian forest*, WA Hamer, Melbourne, 1930. http://digital.slv.vic.gov.au/view/action.

Völuspá: The Seeress's Prophecy, Nick Richardson (trans.), 2014. http://thejunket.org/2014/01/archive/voluspa-the-seeresss-prophecy/.

Watson, Don, *The Bush: Travels in rural Australia*, Hamish Hamilton, Melbourne, 2016.

Wohlleben, Peter, *The Hidden Life of Trees: What they feel, how they communicate—Discoveries from a secret world*, Black Inc., Carlton, 2016.

Woolf, Virginia, *To the Lighthouse*, The Hogarth Press, London, 1927.

Woolf, Virginia, *The Death of the Moth and Other Essays,* The Hogarth Press, London, 1942.

Zipes, Jack, *Grimm Legacies: The magic spell of the Grimms' folk and fairy tales*, Princeton University Press, Princeton University, NJ, 2015.

Articles and Websites

Author Unknown, 'A Seeress from Fyrkat?', National Museum of Denmark. https://en.natmus.dk/historical-knowledge/denmark/prehistoric-period-until-1050-ad/the-viking-age/religion-magic-death-and-rituals/a-seeress-from-fyrkat/.

Author Unknown, 'Ayahuasca', Alcohol and Drug Foundation, 18 May 2020. https://adf.org.au/drug-facts/ayahuasca/.

Author Unknown, 'Christian Hendrik Persoon. Biographical note'. http://www.mushroomthejournal.com/greatlakesdata/Authors/Persoon21.html.

Author Unknown, Entry on Joseph Anderson Panton's *Government Residence, Melbourne, 1837* (1880), State Library Victoria catalogue.

Author Unknown, Entry on Thomas Clark, *Emerald Hill and Sandridge from the Government Domain* (1857), State Library Victoria catalogue.

Author Unknown, 'Jerusalem Olive Trees Among Oldest in the World', 10 October 2012. https://www.abc.net.au/news/2012-10-20/jerusalem-olivetrees-among-oldest-in-world/4324342.

Author Unknown, 'Lyndall Ryan, Mapping the Massacres of Australia's Colonial Frontier', University of Newcastle, 5 July 2017. https://www.newcastle.edu.au/newsroom/featured-news/mapping-the-massacres-of-australias-colonial-frontier.

Author Unknown, 'Six Million Years of African Savanna', National Science Foundation, 3 August 2011. https://www.nsf.gov/news/news_summ.jsp?cntn_id=121029.

Balter, Michael, 'Trees Survived Ice Age Chill in Scandinavia', *Science*, 1 March 2012. http://www.sciencemag.org/news/2012/03/trees-survived-ice-age-chillscandinavia. 1 March 2012.

Birch, Tony, 'Walking and Being', *Meanjin*, Summer 2019. https://meanjin.com.au/essays/walking-and-being.

Bongers, Frans et al., 'Frankincense in Peril', Nature Sustainability, vol. 2, 2019, pp. 602–10.

Bonner, Sarah, 'Visualising Little Red Riding Hood', *Moveable Type*, vol. 2, 'The Mind's Eye', University College, London, 2006. https://discovery.ucl.ac.uk/id/eprint/1572292/1/Sarah%20Bonner.pdf.

Breyer, Melissa, 'Vikings Cleared the Forests, Now Iceland Is Bringing Them Back', *Tree Hugger*, 11 October 2018. https://www.treehugger.com/conservation/vikings-cleared-forests-now-iceland-finally-growing-new-ones.html.

Coder, Kim D, 'Falling Tree Leaves: Leaf abscission', University of Georgia, 1999. http://www.walterreeves.com/uploads/pdf/fallingtreeleavesleafabscission.pdf.

Coghlan, Andy, 'Trees Seen Resting Branches while "Asleep" for the First Time', *New Scientist*, 18 May 2016. https://www.newscientist.com/article/2088833-trees-seen-resting-branches-while-asleep-for the first time.

Collins, Kathryn M, Owen F Price and Trent D Penman, 'Spatial Patterns of Wildfire Ignitions in South-Eastern Australia', *International Journal of Wildland Fire*, vol. 24, no. 8, 2015. https://doi.org/10.1071/WF15054.

Cumming, Ed, 'Who Will Save the Frankincense Tree?', *Daily Telegraph*, 23 December 2012. http://www.telegraph.co.uk/gardening/gardeningadvice/9758581/What-will-save-the-frankincense-tree.html.

Das, Snigdha, 'Plants Have a Lot More than Five Senses', *Nagaland Today*, 3 January 2019. https://nagalandtoday.in/news/2019/01/plants-have-a-lot-more-than-five-senses/.

Dickens, Charles 'Old Lamps for New Ones', *Household Words*, no. 12, 15 June 1850, pp. 12–14. From http://www.engl.duq.edu/servus/PR_Critic/HW15jun50.html. Cited in https://en.wikipedia.org/wiki/Christ_in_the_House_of_His_Parents.

Feltman, Rachel, 'This Tree Might Be the Oldest Living Thing in Europe', *The Washington Post*, 19 August 2016. https://www.washingtonpost.com/news/speaking-of-science/wp/2016/08/19/this-tree-might-be-the-oldest-livingthing-in-europe/.

Freud, Sigmund, 'A Disturbance of Memory on the Acropolis' (1936), *The Standard Edition of the Complete Psychological Works of Sigmund Freud*, in James Strachey (ed. and trans.) in collaboration with Anna Freud, The Hogarth Press, London, 1962, vol. XXII.

Freud, Sigmund, 'Mourning and Melancholia' (1917), *The Standard Edition of the Complete Psychological Works of Sigmund Freud*, in James Strachey (ed. and trans.) in collaboration with Anna Freud, The Hogarth Press, London, 1957, vol. XIV.

Freud, Sigmund, 'Screen Memories' (1899), *The Standard Edition of the Complete Psychological Works of Sigmund Freud*, in James Strachey (ed. and trans.) in collaboration with Anna Freud, The Hogarth Press, London, 1974, vol. III.

Gibson, Miranda, 'I Spent 449 Days in a Tree Without Touching the Ground—It Was All Worth It', *The Guardian*, 25 June 2013. https://www.theguardian.com/commentisfree/2013/jun/25/tasmania-tree-protest-logging.

Haines, Gavin, 'How Iceland Re-created a Viking-Age Religion', *BBC Travel*, 3 June 2019. http://www.bbc.com/travel/story/20190602-how-iceland-recreated-a-viking-age-religion.

Hoh, Amanda, 'Christmas Tree Farmer Braces for the Silly Season and Offers Tips to Make Your Tree Last', 5 December 2016. http://www.abc.net.au/news/2016-12-05/how-to-take-care-of-your-christmas-tree/8092810.

Illing, Sean, 'The Brutal Mirror: What the psychedelic drug ayahuasca showed me about my life', first published 19 February 2018. https://www.vox.com/first-person/2018/2/19/16739386/ayahuasca-retreat-psychedelic-hallucination-meditation.

Jakobsen, Rasmus Kragh, 'Trees Survived the Ice Age in Scandinavia', Science Nordic, 2 March 2012. http://sciencenordic.com/trees-survived-ice-age-scandinavia.

Jean, Lydie, 'Charles Perrault's Paradox: How aristocratic fairy tales became synonymous with folklore conservation', Trames, vol. 11, (61/56), no. 3, 2007. https://kirj.ee/public/trames/ref-tr-07-3-3.htm.

Kent, Rachel, 'After Nature', in Rachel Kent (ed.), Janet Laurence After Nature, Museum of Contemporary Art Australia, Sydney, 2019.

Londoño, Ernesto, Manuela Andreon and Letícia Casado, 'Amazon Deforestation Soars as Pandemic Hobbles Enforcement', The New York Times, 6 June 2020. https://www.nytimes.com/2020/06/06/world/americas/amazon-deforestation-brazil.html.

Loomis, Ilima, 'Trees in the Amazon Make Their Own Rain', Science, 4 August 2017. https://www.sciencemag.org/news/2017/08/trees-amazon-make-their-own-rain.

Macnab, Geoffrey, 'Deepa Mehta: A director in deep water—all over again', The Independent, 19 May 2006. https://www.independent.co.uk/arts-entertainment/films/features/deepa-mehta-a-director-in-deep-water-all-over-again-478731.html.

Murray, Melissa, Wedge-Tailed Eagle, Australian National Museum website. https://australian.museum/learn/animals/birds/wedge-tailed-eagle/.

Narasimhan, N, 'Beyond Widowhood, for a Life of Fulfilment', The Hindu, 10 September 2017. https://www.thehindu.com/opinion/open-page/beyond-widowhood-for-a-life-of-fulfilment/article19651236.ece.

O'Brien, ME, H Anderson, E Kaukel, K O'Byrne, M Pawlicki, J Von Pawel and M Reck, 'SRL172 (Killed Mycobacterium Vaccae) in Addition to Standard Chemotherapy Improves Quality of Life Without Affecting Survival, in Patients with Advanced Non-Small-Cell Lung Cancer: Phase III results', PubMed.Gov., 2004. https://pubmed.ncbi.nlm.nih.gov/15151947/.

Odell, Amy, 'Has PETA Finally Won the War Against Fur?', The Cut, 1 October 2018. https://www.thecut.com/2018/10/has-peta-finally-won-the-war-against-fur.html.

Ollerton, Jeff, 'Biological Barter: Patterns of specialisation compared across different mutualisms', in Nickolas M Waser and Jeff Ollerton (eds), Plant-pollinator Interactions: From specialization to generalization, University of Chicago Press, 2006. https://www.researchgate.net/publication/269277177_Biological_Barter_patterns_of_specialization_compared_across_different_mutualisms.

Pandey, Kirti, 'How to Do Vat Savitri Puja', Times Now News, 22 May 2020. https://www.timesnownews.com/spiritual/religion/article/how-to-do-vat-savitri-puja-pooja-procedure-vat-savitri-vrat-katha/594380.

Pattanaik, Devdutt, 'When a Man Loves a Woman', 6 January 2019. https://devdutt.com/articles/when-a-man-loves-a-woman/.

Phillips, Richard and Waruna Alahakoon, 'Hindu Chauvinists Block Filming of Deepa Mehta's Water', World Socialist Web Site, 12 February 2000. https://www.wsws.org/en/articles/2000/02/film-f12.html.

Powell, Eric A, 'Telling Tales in Proto-Indo-European', Archaeology, n.d. https://www.archaeology.org/exclusives/articles/1302-proto-indo-european-schleichers-fable.

Raffaele, Paul, 'Sleeping with Cannibals', Smithsonian Magazine, September 2006. http://www.smithsonianmag.com/travel/sleeping-with-cannibals-128958913/#yDsEb2tgEkajeOHD.99.

Robbins, Jim, 'Chronicles of the Rings: What trees tell us', The New York Times, 30 April 2019. https://www.nytimes.com/2019/04/30/science/tree-rings-climate.html.

Rønsted, Nina, George D Weiblen, V Savolainen and James M Cook, 'Phylogeny, Biogeography and Ecology of Ficus Section Malvanthera (Moraceae)', Molecular

Phylogenetics and Evolution, vol. 48, no. 1, 2008. https://www.sciencedirect.com/science/article/pii/S1055790308001528.

Ryan, Lyndall, 'Billibellary, the Formation of the Native Police Force in the Port Phillip District in 1837 and Its Connection to the Batman Treaty of 1835', *Law and History*, vol. 4, no. 2, 2017.

Sahsnotasvriunt, Tyra Alrune, 'Yggdrasil—Yew not Ash Tree'. https://paganmeltingpot.wordpress.com/2014/09/17/yggdrasil-yew-not-Ash-tree/.

Sayers, Andrew, 'Tommy McRae', *Australian Dictionary of Biography*. http://adb.anu.edu.au/biography/mcrae-tommy-13074.

Sendy, Matt, '"The Amazon is Completely Lawless": The rainforest after Bolsonaro's first year', *The New York Times*, 5 December 2019. https://www.nytimes.com/2019/12/05/world/americas/amazon-fires-bolsonaro-photos.html.

Siddal, Liv, 'Spiritual Dimensions—A Visit to the Site of Iceland's New Pagan Temple', 1 June 2015. https://www.itsnicethat.com/articles/iceland-pagan-temple.

Smith, Lydia, 'City of Widows: The 38,000 forgotten women of Varanasi', *International Business Times*, 30 June 2015. https://www.ibtimes.co.uk/city-widows-38000-forgotten-women-varanasi-1505560.

Stasch, Rupert, 'Korowai Treehouses and the Everyday Representation of Time, Belonging and Death', *The Asia Pacific Journal of Anthropology*, vol. 12, no. 4, August 2011.

Summerly, Victoria, 'A Retreat of One's Own: Tending to Virginia Woolf's country plot proved a surprising insight into the writer herself', *The Independent*, 19 October 2013. https://www.independent.co.uk/property/gardening/a-retreat-of-ones-own-tending-to-virginia-woolfs-country-plot-proved-a-surprising-insight-into-the-8884225.html.

Sweney, Mark, 'BBC Admits Treehouse Scene from Human Planet Series Was Faked', *The Guardian*, 4 April 2018. https://www.theguardian.com/media/2018/apr/04/scene-from-human-planet-documentary-was-faked-bbc-admits.

Taylor, Leslie, 'Bellaco Caspi', Rain-Tree Publishers, n.d. https://rain-tree.com/himatanthus.htm.

Tengberg, Margareta, 'Beginnings and Early History of Date Palm Garden Cultivation in the Middle East', *Journal of Arid Environments*, vol. 86, November 2012. https://www.sciencedirect.com/science/article/pii/S0140196311003569#!.

Than, Ker, 'World's First Tree Reconstructed', *Live Science*, 18 April 2007. http://www.livescience.com/1439-world-tree-reconstructed.html.

The Observer Tree. https://observertree.org/about/.

Woolf, Virginia, 'In the Orchard', 1923. https://lithub.com/in-the-orchard/.

Film

Gagliano, Monica, www.youtube.com/watch?v=90BUQoLu_Hg, 26 November 2018.

Miranda Gibson, documentary, 2014, director Jeff Wirth. https://www.youtube.com/watch?v=Q26PNqyxIm4.

The Tree, feature film, 2010, director and writer Julie Bertuccelli, produced by Sue Taylor, Yaël Fogiel and Laetitia Gonzalez, Taylor Media/Les Films du Poisson.

Water, feature film, 2005, director and writer Deepa Mehta, screenplay Anurag Kashyap, produced by David Hamilton.

Poetry

Williams, William Carlos, 'Winter Trees', 1921. https://www.poets.org/poetsorg/poem/winter-trees. Online text copyright © 2003, Ian Lancashire for the Department of English, University of Toronto.

Acknowledgements

I'd like to sincerely thank the following for various forms of advice and assistance during my research:

Patrick Baker, Professor of Silviculture and Forest Ecology, University of Melbourne; Su Baker, Pro Vice-Chancellor, Community and Cultural Partnerships, University of Melbourne; Renee Beale, Royal Society of Victoria; Dale Dixon, Collections Manager, Royal Botanic Gardens and Domain Trust, Brisbane; Robyn Eckersly, Professor of Social and Political Sciences, University of Melbourne; Meyer Eidelson; Elizabeth Gower; Isaac Herman; Walter Johnson, Winthrop Professor of History and Professor of African and African American Studies, Harvard University; Florence M Jumonville, Earl K Long Library, University of New Orleans; Dan Kehlman, Plant Identification and Advisory Services, Queensland Herbarium; Rachel Kent, Senior Curator, Museum of Contemporary Art Australia, Sydney; Janet Laurence; Allan Milburn, Wycheproof Historical Society; Neil and Zaylee, Port Phillip EcoCentre; Sally K Reeves, Office of the Clerk of Civil District Court for the Parish of Orleans; Carol Siegel, Director, Freud Museum London; Katherine Vollen, National Archives, Washington DC; Phyllis and Jim Wagner.

Thanks also to the enthusiastic members and citizen scientists of the Elsternwick Park Association.

And to Gordon Blake, devotee of the Moreton Bay Fig.

I'm deeply grateful to the Literature Board, Australia Council for the Arts and the Centre of Visual Art, University of Melbourne, for the funding that made sections of this research possible.

The team at Melbourne University Publishing—Nathan Hollier, Louise Stirling, Meaghan Amor and Eugenie Baulch—provided a fantastically supportive environment for the publication process.

Index

(Note: Page locators in italics indicate illustration)

This book was designed and typeset by
Pfisterer + Freeman and Cannon Typesetting
The text was set in 12 point Bembo
with 15 points of leading
The text was printed on 100 gsm Woodfree
This book was edited by Meaghan Amor

THE
MIEGUNYAH
PRESS